David R. Bengtson

Past Lives of Famous People
Journeys of the Soul

David R. Bengtson

Past Lives of
Famous People

Journeys of the Soul

Bluestar
Communications®

Woodside, California

AwC
133.90135
Beng
15.95

© 1997 David R. Bengtson

Published by:
Bluestar Communications Corporation
44 Bear Glenn
Woodside, CA 94062
Tel: 800-6-Bluestar

Edited by Jude Berman
Cover Art by Garret Moore, Dreaming Lizard Studios
Layout: Petra Michel

Copyright Cover Illustration:
© 1997 Garret Moore & Bluestar Communications Corporation
First printing 1997
ISBN: 1-885394-22-5

Library of Congress Cataloging-in-Publication Data
Bengtson, David R., 1944-
Past lives of famous people : journeys of the soul / David R. Bengtson.
p. cm.
Includes index.
ISBN 1-885394-22-5
1. Reincarnation. 2. Akashic records. 3. Celebrities--Miscellanea. I. Title
BF1045.A44B46 1997
133.9'01'35--dc21   97-9116
                                                                      CIP

The contents of this book are based solely on the imagination and musings of the author, who does not intend any implication, suggestion or conclusion about the actual character, personality, traits, beliefs or behavior of the highly visible public figures, past and present, who are named herein.

Printed in USA

Contents

5

7

Publisher's Preface

As a publisher of primarily New Age literature, I am continually confronted with the latest "revelations" about who was who in former lives. It is often difficult, if not impossible, to discern truth from fiction. For this reason, I have chosen in the past not to publish books with specific revelations.

However, this book by David Bengtson is unique because its revelations are presented as tools to illustrate how karma and the reincarnation of souls work in a broader historical context. The author does not claim to be correct with respect to individual cases, but rather encourages readers to study these cases and draw their own conclusions.* This is especially important because some of these cases involve well-known celebrities who are still alive. Again and again, the author points out that his studies are not meant as judgments, but as a means to understand the flow of history through the ages.

I, too, would like to invite you to follow David Bengtson's thoughts and to enter a journey that might grant you some new insight into historic events. But keep in mind: "Examine everything, but keep only the best."

Petra Michel
Bluestar Communications

---

* The contents of this book are based solely on the imagination and musings of the author, who does not intend any implication, suggestion or conclusion about the actual character, personality, traits, beliefs or behavior of the highly visible public figures, past and present, who are named herein.

Author's Preface

Greetings! You are hereby invited to come on an adventurous trek through time.

With this presentation on the subject of reincarnation and the Akashic Records, I would like to offer you an opportunity to review new perspectives on one of life's most interesting mysteries, as well as to revisit some intuitive ideas that may not have occurred to you (in this lifetime) until now. For example, if reincarnation is actually a divine principle of life, how has its activity been expressed throughout history? Do only souls reincarnate, or do entire civilizations return to live again?

When approaching a subject such as this, we must realize that we are not discussing knowledge as much as we are speaking about vision and intuition. What the soul's eye—or higher intuitive mind—sees cannot always be interpreted in obvious ways.

Ever controversial, the question also remains whether the past lives of living persons should be made public—and what the karmic consequences of that would be. The standard applied here is to openly discuss only those who are very famous public figures. Some well-known personalities have chosen to become public icons and, as such, can serve in a similar capacity on a spiritual level as public examples for the study of reincarnation.

It must be remembered that this work is the product of meditative insight.

The result of any type of meditative contemplation is best approached with a gentle spirit. The opinions expressed in this work are meant to stimulate spiritual study and learning; any commentaries, especially those that reflect on the lives of living persons, are not intended to cause harm to anyone, nor to expose personal details or faults. The revealing of past lives in this manner can, and does, have an educational purpose. As students of Akashic history and the inner life, those of us who are learning to view our present time as a platform of living history, have the right to share our insights with others and to discuss our vision of the collective social condition. This includes insights into the past lives of famous personalities on both sides of the veil of life.

With careful reflection, it is clear that what affects our collective humanity moment-by-moment (at least from the perspective of reincarnation) depends on, and results from, past events involving the reincarnation of millions of individuals. History is not only something that happened a long time ago—history is now. We exist in a living, moving, transforming theater of historical events that influence us on many levels, both material and spiritual. Becoming more aware of this can add to our sense of social and spiritual connection to others across time.

This presentation, including the introductory material and various past-life case studies that follow, is meant to be read sequentially. Each case study contributes to the next, as well as to the whole, in an orderly manner; therefore, reading slowly through, from the introduction to the last biography—at least on the first read—is the best way to experience this offering. Because of the importance of this sequential ordering for the subject matter, the table of contents and the alphabetical list of names should only be used for general reference.

As you progress through these studies, it will become obvious that some of the biographies are merely skeleton presentations. You may notice, in some cases, jumps of ideation or assumptions that linger unexplained. In other cases, you will find that questions or answers are offered, yet something obvious remains unexplained. This is intentional. Some of the case studies are presented only as aids, indicators or road markers that can contribute to the discovery, contemplation and understanding of cultural progression. In several cases, no particular attempt has been made to give a full biographical overview of the subject; in such cases, material that seems incomplete must be viewed as a prompt for further research or meditation on the part of the student. This entire work must be viewed as an overview of a subject so vast that many lifetimes could be spent at the doorway of introduction.

I wish to give special thanks to all those who helped bring this basic text into existence, especially my wife Denise, whose constant encouragement and efforts in biographical research made this presentation possible at this time.

Our work is dedicated to fellow students who seek the way of higher learning. To all with the courage to persevere on the path of truth, may the light of God guide you safely through the halls of Akashia.

David Bengtson
Escondido, California, November 1996

12

Introduction

Many of us, young and old, self-educated or academic, have an interest in the origins of our society, in our respective cultures and in the common conditions of our time. History, after all, is common property; anyone with an interest in this subject is therefore invited to explore with us the influence of reincarnation through time.

In the course of our study, we will re-examine the progress of individuals, of groups, of families, of entire peoples and nations, from one century to the next. We will review the record of life as through a window in inner consciousness, to be understood as a moving play, a grand panorama presenting one long, continuous dramatic action. The Akashic Record is an inner recording, or memory of life, that is written in the cosmic ethers. To some, it appears as a moving thought-picture, or thought-form, containing impressions of past and present life on earth. Learning to interpret this record is a fascinating experience. In this presentation, the reader is invited to explore with us a small portion of this vast subject, presented in the form of insights into the past lives of famous people.

My own personal first contact with the record of past lives occurred almost thirty years ago, at the age of nineteen. It happened as follows.

A friend with whom I had grown up was accepted at the University of California at Berkeley. A few months after he left our community, this friend was traveling with three others, all eighteen and nineteen years old, all possibly drunk, on the expressway in San Francisco. An accident took place in front of these boys and their car was forced off the road, about forty or fifty meters above ground level. The top of their car was sheared off and all four of the young college students were decapitated.

When I heard about the accident, I was devastated.

Two or three months after this event, I had what I have learned to call an *epic dream*, or a *dream of substance*. I have always been able to tell the difference between an ordinary dream and one that touches a deeper reality. In this particular dream, I found myself observing a group of four young men sitting at a table in a tavern. I was aware that this tavern was in France, and that it was at the time of the French Revolution. These four young men were not poor. Although they came from aristocratic families, they had joined in the revolution with great fervor, as had many of the aristocratic youth of that time.

As I observed, the four young French aristocrats in the tavern became rowdy and jovial. I watched them raise their glasses for a toast. They were quite drunk. One man said, "Vive la revolution!" Another said, "Vive!" And another said, "…and if they will not, then off with their heads!" Then all four of them said, "Yes, off with their heads!" They all tipped their cups together with a solid, clicking sound.

As their cups came together in that fervent toast, the dream transmuted itself. Suddenly, I saw the vision of the automobile on the expressway in California with those same young men in it. These four men had come together again, this time in an American life. Their opportunity to obtain wealth and privilege had been renewed. However, shortly after they had been accepted at the university, their car careened off the expressway and all four of *their* heads were taken off in the accident.

14

I awoke from that dream with a feeling that it represented some deep meaning. I have given a great deal of thought to that sleeping vision. It helped me, at the beginning of my studies, understand the power of what is called *karma*—the power of life balancing itself, of former thought and feeling fulfilling itself.

At that young age, I had already developed an interest in spiritual studies. Although I had not yet achieved significant depth in my studies, this epic vision initiated me into a new level of desire to understand. I began to take my spiritual studies more seriously. I came to accept that the will of God was manifest in that accident, and I was able to let go of the sense of loss and pain for my friend.

The path of spiritual awareness that I have followed has always been a path of Christian mysticism emphasizing prayer and communion with God. In contrast with the opinion of most Christian churches, I did not find my evolving interest in reincarnation and past lives to be in conflict with my being Christian. It is my belief that Christianity should be a holistic, universal approach to higher spiritual truth and reality that includes many levels of understanding.

In the spring of 1968, at age 23, I was fortunate enough to be led to a fine teacher, the Reverend Flower A. Newhouse—a Californian, New Age Christian minister and mystic who possessed a high degree of spiritual clairvoyance.[1] This Christian pastor was able to see, and interpret, the inner light auras of plants, animals and people; she also talked of visions of saints, angels and devic nature beings from the invisible, higher dimensional planes. She taught with authority about her direct conscious experience of the Christ and of spiritual guidance from higher worlds. Flower Newhouse also demonstrated an ability to read the Akashic Records from a higher perspective. In her public lectures, she often commented on historical events and spiritual truths that were revealed in the Akashic Records.

In 1969 and in the early 1970s, I had several private interviews with Flower Newhouse, during which I had an opportunity to ask her about the visions that had been coming to me both in lucid dreams and in conscious meditation. These personal interviews were very pleasant and interesting to me. Flower (as we called her) had an open and inquisitive mind. She was eager to share her experiences and was interested in the inner experiences of others. Several things that she revealed to me at that time concerning other lives, I have since been able to confirm.

I do not consider these details to be public information; however, as personal testimony offered to fellow students, for the purpose of the development of this work, I will reveal some of what Flower communicated to me at that time. Please remember that I have had an opportunity to think about these things for over twenty-five years.

One of the first things that Flower mentioned in our initial interview was that she could see the symbol of a shell in my aura.

---

[1] Flower A. Newhouse and her husband Lawrence Newhouse are the founders of Questhaven Retreat in Southern California.

She described it as a type that was earned by persons who had—in some life, or in some dramatic way—sacrificed themselves for the truth. "That is how I know that you are truthful," she said. "This shell symbol is placed in the aura of a student by a higher spiritual teacher, angel or spiritual master to communicate to those who can see that this person is truthful."

"You possess a natural ability to recognize the difference between good and evil," she commented. "You have good intuitive discernment and will be able to help others in this area. This is what the symbol of the shell signifies."

This information confirmed for me why the intuitive recognition of who is who, or what is what, has usually come easily and naturally to me—and has usually proven to be correct over time.

Flower also volunteered comments on three past lives of importance to me (which I have since confirmed). She had known me, she said, in two of these lives. The first was as a student in the school of Pythagoras; the second was in a life as a young Greek disciple of Jesus. Meditation on this lifetime with Jesus has had the most meaning for me, although I still have not completely detached that awareness from a sense of the trauma of the cross.

"I remember you well in that life in Palestine," Flower told me. "You were young, well-educated, of foreign origin, from a Greek merchant family. You were quiet and reserved, choosing to remain in the outer circle, listening and asking few questions. You were with the followers for at least three years before the crucifixion. You were designated as one of the seventy who were to go out to start missions—which you did. You lived out a long life, becoming an elder or abbot of a mission house on the road from Jerusalem, some miles south of Antioch, where early Christian family members could stop and rest. You would share your memories of Jesus with them. You were well-known and well-loved among those of the early Church, living to an age of at least eighty."

Flower also referred to other lives in my past, including one as a soldier/teacher in the early Frankish empire, during the time of Charlemagne. None of these lives has historical fame. I told her

of other visions and glimpses of the past that had come to me—
none, however, as emotionally traumatic as the life with Jesus. It
was at this time that Flower confirmed that I could develop the
ability, of which I was already becoming aware, to do past-life
studies. She told me that I was an *Akashic Records specialist* in
my higher Self. How much of this ability I would develop in this
lifetime she couldn't say, but she did say that this was who I was
inwardly. This ability to work with the Akashic Records would,
in time, manifest as my spiritual gift and specialty of service to
others. I feel that her prediction is correct. What I love most is to
share stories of revealed memories. Since those interviews with
Flower twenty-five years ago, I can say this much: revisiting history has indeed become my favorite pastime.

Over the years, I have continued to pursue a normal life—
marrying, having children, and working as an artisan in the field
of construction. I also continued to attend as many of Flower's
lectures as possible. And, in whatever time was available, I have
conducted my historical studies. An intense interest in history, in
historical events and in historical personages continued to develop in me.

In my meditations, I slowly began to be able to precipitate
conscious visions of a type similar to my original dream. I stimulated visions by concentrating on a thought or question. I found,
in time, that I was able to think deeply, meditate deeply and then
penetrate into past events. With practice, my vision opened up
more as I meditated prior to sleep. On occasion, I could see panoramic events taking place before my sight, a process that is almost identical to looking into a television image. I could see faces,
persons and events of an historical nature.

My vision experiences were almost impossible to control at
first. I would just observe. Eventually, I discovered that the capacity to observe events or persons could be enhanced by meditation that was focused on the individual or event. This method
allowed me to link people to other lives. And I learned to discern
the qualities of the connection between observed faces and actual events. Identifying time in these moving scenes was (and
still is) an interesting and complex challenge. It was necessary to

17

learn to "read" the record—which can best be described as a mental immersion in "knowing." As I practiced this, I realized that I was receiving help from an angel. This higher form of help was necessary to enable my connection between the inner "knower" and the outer self.

Since that time, which is now more than twenty years ago, I have been keeping notes, and my notebooks have grown into a substantial collection. Personally, I don't feel a need to publish. However, I know that, at the age of twenty, I myself would have appreciated discovering this collection of work. For this reason, I'm offering this work to anyone who loves history and wants to learn to discern history from a higher perspective. Here is an opportunity to exercise, and perhaps further develop, intuitive mental capacities. These commentaries are offered as assistance to students interested in this type of work. This is a gift of learning and of experience—no more, no less. In that spirit it is offered. If Akashic history interests you, you are welcome to proceed into the higher worlds, and into the halls of learning.

Basic Principles

20

The Higher Worlds

The higher worlds are spiritual realms that, whether we are conscious of it or not, we live in continually—realms of soul being. These are the worlds known as "heaven," or "paradise," that the higher Self never leaves. The higher Self, our innermost Self, is closely related to the world of consciousness, and is consciously active in the inner dimensions. It is in these realms that our souls are immortal. This is the truth behind the words of Jesus: "I believe in the resurrection and the life."

In the state between lives, after one life is over, we return as an individual form to a conscious existence in the higher worlds. It is in this inner individuality that different lives merge in memory. As we reincarnate, the memory of past lives is retained by the higher Self.

Higher soul energy does not typically incarnate in its fullness here on earth. However, channels to the higher realms can be opened by spiritual means, so that true spiritual energy can penetrate into this earth plane. It can come through a pure life, the life of a saint or the life of a spiritual master. Such was the life of Jesus, wherein the light shown purely through his person while he was here in the world.

Spiritual Drama

From the perspective of higher spiritual reality, the life that we are living now is a dream experience—a scripted performance. Is it not healthy to regard life as a performance, a kind of soul circus? Viewing our participation in growth and learning as a psychodrama allows us to focus more easily on the karmic characteristics of each life pattern.

To begin to know the truth of life, we can adopt the perspective that our personality is just a stage part, another role that we have been assigned, or that we have chosen to play, in the endless passion of life. For example, when a great actor plays a part in the theater, that part does not cause any stain or negativity for the actor. The part only deepens the actor's skills. Whether the part is one of great joy or great sadness, one of great power or great poverty, the performer only grows through his participation.

Of all the many spiritual teachings made throughout secular history, none is more profound than Shakespeare's statement: "All of life is but a stage, and we are but actors upon it." I believe that, in a collective way, all of life is a great spiritual performance. Human social interaction is the great play of history and culture, including the innumerable dramas of individual, family, tribal and community life.

From this point of view, our personal self in this lifetime is only part of a greater universal drama. Such a perspective allows us to develop a healthy degree of impersonal separation. With this viewpoint, no matter what karmic condition we find ourselves in, we can learn from it.

Nor is it entirely a passive game. It is possible for us, once we become somewhat aware of the spiritual life, to affect the script and even to upgrade it. This is possible within the conditions that life offers us. If no effort is made, we simply live out the role we were born into. This psychodrama can continue for families, as well as individuals.

Karmic Condition

Within the spiritual drama, some lives are lived as payment for a serious debt. To reverse a previously faulty or destructive set of choices, one who has burned witches may become a defense attorney; one who supported a racist movement may incarnate as the member of a beleaguered minority race. This is called a *karmic condition*.

Judgment, however, must be withheld, especially when trying to understand karmic conditions. Wisdom, in this case, is an earned condition of receptive understanding, supported by open-mindedness. Open-mindedness can begin with doubt. Healthy doubt leads to the honest kind of research that is necessary for learning. Therefore, whenever intellectual or spiritual struggle is necessary, let doubt be your servant, even as truth is your guide.

The Repetition Compulsion

Why does one person suffer? Why does another profit? Why does one fail? Why does yet another succeed?

These kinds of questions help us understand the nature of karmic consequence—the movement from one life to another. A link exists between the soul and each of the parts it plays in different lifetimes. This is especially true in the absence of any conscious awareness of a spiritual path, a path of redemption or of salvation.

Salvation means coming into the consciousness of the light and love of God. One who is on the path of spiritual enlightenment may be able to transform the relationship between the soul and the part it plays in life. However, personalities who are not on a conscious spiritual path will find themselves bound more tightly to the earth. Matter binds such people more and more tightly to the roles they play, until their souls are able to bring at least some awareness of the divine light of immortality into their lives.

A certain magnetism often exists in a group that recognizes those individuals who have been great performers in collectively shared past-life dramas. These individuals are drawn forward with such unconscious messages as: "This one has been our king." "This one has been our spiritual leader." "This one has been the great explorer." "Should we now support him in his new venture?" "Should we vote for this person now that we are struggling with problems of democracy?" "Should we elect this person who was once before our emperor?" When it comes time for the election, who is it who stands up and proclaims, "I volunteer"? Of course, this would be the tendency, even the compulsion, of those people who have already had the karma of leading the group.

It is a two-sided matter. Individuals may recognize their karma and interpret it as their *dharma* or duty. At the same time, the collective—whether it is collective karma or collective curiosity—tends to call these persons into the forefront. This phenomena is known as *repetition compulsion.* For some, the same psychospiritual scripts are played over and over, life after life after life—with a constant compulsion to repeat, to repeat, to repeat.

It has been my observation that persons who are not firmly on a spiritual path tend to unconsciously engage in repetition compulsion, often repeating another life exactly, step by step. On the other hand, those who are becoming more spiritually aware have a tendency to depart from repetition compulsion. Such individuals may do things quite differently once they have taken more conscious control of their lives. Becoming conscious of, and getting control of, repetition is one of the struggles of our moral life. In fact, it is the work of our higher Self.

Soul Life

It is important to remember that we are always free and immortal in our divine higher Self. We are born into this life to make of it what we can, to learn what we can. However, our true, eternal life is that of our divine higher Self within higher worlds.

When we reach the point at which we are able to contemplate our own past incarnations, how that life relates to another life becomes significant. It is essential to realize that who we are today, in *persona*, has never lived before. Our outward personality, in its particular expression, lives only one life.

The persona is the temporary mask that we use for the various parts that we play. However, it is important to recognize that we are both persona and an extension of soul consciousness at the same time. Soul consciousness can remember other personalities, other parts that we have played in other lives. You, as this personality, are not that other personality, but your soul has experienced that other personality as well as you. It is a subtle differentiation.

This truth about soul life is often taught at the preliminary levels of the inner worlds. Those who return from near-death experiences, for example, and report that they were told that reincarnation does not exist, are reporting accurately. Reincarnation applies at the soul level, not at the level of the persona. As a result, the principle of reincarnation may not always be clearly understood in the lower strata of the spirit world.

The Halls of Learning

As we go deeper into our study of the higher realms and of the Akashic Records, we naturally begin to wish for greater understanding. At this point, we are likely to visit the inner planes, which are found between sleeping and waking, and to attend a hall of learning. In these higher places of learning, we use the vision and intuition of the higher Self to see with more perfect clarity. In the higher levels of the inner worlds, we can function with relatively unlimited powers of intuition, unhampered by purely earth-bound consciousness. As we become more aware of the reality of reincarnation and past lives in our outer life, a deeper connection is made with the soul. Communication and comprehension take place with much greater speed.

A place exists in the higher spiritual dimensions where we as a group are gathering to do this work. I have had several dreams and visions of standing in an auditorium delivering a lecture to a large group of people. These visions are of a higher dimensional reality. The walls of this other-dimensional auditorium seem to be circular, in the shape of a 360-degree screen. At least a couple of hundred people are seated there. A panorama, or moving picture, is projected around us, expressing visions of historical events and persons. The images correspond to the group's mental focus during our discussion.

How the form of this study hall appears to different people probably depends somewhat on the level of each person's mental projections. As the whole group participates collectively in the discussion, the pictures on the screen change. In this way, the group is able to follow the presentation through a kind of group-enhanced mental clairvoyance, with the images actually appearing to be projected on a large circular screen.

A student's presence in the inner school may be unconscious to his or her outer persona. Nevertheless, during a discussion in the higher realms, similar to a question and answer session, any imperfections in his or her understanding are corrected. Such inquiries take on a group significance. Together, the collective mind of the group concentrates on the panoramic vision of history. We are able to obtain greater focus as a group, which facilitates answers to our questions. Collectively, we know the questions and we know the answers. We are able to retain our learning from this inner-plane presentation, which then feeds our intuition in the waking state.

As far as I can tell, the main requirement for attendance in this hall of learning is a person's desire to be there. We must develop and nurture a desire to "know," or to "learn," through the guidance of our higher Self. This higher type of desire tends to take priority over other, lower desires and interests.

In order to actually get into the hall of learning, an open mind is also important. If a person is not open to the concept of Akashic history then, of course, its study is not open to that person. Whether on the inner planes or the outer side of life, a person whose mind is too closed would not be able to achieve inner community with the halls of learning. An interest in the subject of history and of historical personalities must be combined with a willingness to study biographical material beyond one's present cultural limits.

Methods

Before we begin to link specific historical lives and to discuss their linkages, I would like to mention that there is more than one approach to the memory of other lives. Our work has to do with Akashic revelation and research. Akashic research has a karmic purpose and does not have the same spiritual energy or purpose that is sometimes used in psychological healing work. However, whether the focus is on karmic revelation or on healing, all spiritual energy comes from the same divine source.

Concerning healing work and the memory of past lives, there is a method of tapping subconscious memory that is used in some circles for psychological healing and that involves guided self-hypnosis. This method is called *past-life regression*. Past-life regression is a deeply personal way to tap into the subconscious mind. This method can be used by qualified therapists who wish to aid patients in recalling traumatic memories associated with early childhood, prenatal or even past-life states of being. Such therapies are now conducted routinely and successfully with many patients worldwide.

In past-life regression therapy, the doctor and patient typically work with fictional psychodrama, and are not concerned about whether the memories that are uncovered have any basis in historically fact. In such therapy, what is important is the healing of emotional trauma. Sometimes, however, a person in such a sensitized semi-trance state of self-observation gains access to the true memory of other lives. It is my opinion that guided hypnotic regression should only be used for healing purposes in trauma patients—if at all.

When trauma emerges from the unconscious, competent help is often needed. Any method of gaining access to the subconscious mind through hypnotic regression is potentially dangerous. Only trained psychologists of high moral character should be trusted to use such methods. This is an important warning, not to be taken lightly.

It is my experience that the personal subconscious does not reach beyond the direct experience of the individual involved. In other words, an individual under the influence of hypnotic regression can only gain access to past-life memories of a personal nature. Memories of events outside those times during which the individual lived are unlikely to be available.

A discriminating student of Akashic research must learn to stay fully conscious while activating the higher intuitive mind through proper meditation. The method that I recommend is only vaguely related to regression hypnosis. I do not support what is sometimes called *psychism*. I do not, for example, use or encourage the use of any unconscious forms of psychic channeling, hypnosis, automatic hand writing or trances. In every case that I am aware of, in which such devices or techniques were used, the researcher or "channel" seems to have gotten off track. A mind that has not begun to stretch the fabric of assumption occasionally "sees" without comprehending what is seen.

In conducting Akashic research, conscious access to the higher planes is similar to healthy mental development. It should be clean, clear, balanced and conscious. It requires intense higher mental focus and dedication.

Where, exactly, is this space that contains the Akashic Records? It is necessary to reach toward a higher zone than the personal subconscious. With right spiritual alignment, prayer and meditation, it is possible to receive inner guidance that can lead you to the Akashic Records.

The method I recommend is concentration on the "space" that contains our collective memory. This is not gained through the personal subconscious, but rather through an impersonal stretching upward and inward in meditation. In this way, it is possible to touch the Akashic Records. This space can be described as a thin, atomic stratum of a multiple-layered substance—etheric, astral, mental and causal. Each of its layers is more clear, true and refined than the one before. The purest layers form a bridge between the worlds.

What may be called the repository of the higher Akashic Records contains everything that has ever happened on earth. This repository includes imprints of times and places that we, as individuals, have not experienced. In as much as we can become one in spirit with God—and with each other—on a higher level, we can also become one with eternal memory, universal and true. Such a thing is not to be feared; truth is the ultimate liberator. As Jesus said, "Know the truth, for the truth shall make you free."

Emotional Biases

Many people who are attracted to this kind of work are already knowledgeable about history. For them, the problem of keeping an open mind may be more difficult than for someone with less academic preparation. Anyone who holds a strong bias, preconception or misconception may be resistant to new perspectives and possibilities.

On an emotional level—and this is often the source of greatest resistance—many well-known historical personalities have been elevated to mythical status as cultural icons. Some people who study this subject become emotionally perplexed when they discover that present culture is not the center of the cultural universe. After all, how can *all* our cultural heroes be expected to move on with another language or cultural wave? Have we been left behind? This is a good question but an unnecessary concern. It is important to release preconceptions about personalities in history; we must be willing to overcome any strong emotional desire to defend assumptions about past lives of famous people.

World history moves forward on a different karmic wave than that of personal need. Wherever a person incarnates on the world plane is perfect for that person's needs. Many historical people move on with a wave of world culture that we can readily identify and understand. However, cultural pride in the mind of an Akashic researcher can prevent inner intuitive perceptions from coming into outer awareness. For example, psychic scars from recent wars or ethnic, racial or religious prejudice can make it difficult for some people to "see" with universal perspective. A good principle of research is this: Always question past assumptions but never block reception of new possibilities.

An Openness to Guidance

The twentieth century has seen a few competent Akashic readers; however, various incorrect assumptions about past lives have been floating around in recent years. Some of the more common errors originated from statements or published remarks made by high-profile psychics. To avoid this, we must learn to reach into the Akashic Records ourselves, and to seek confirmation from the higher realms.

Engaging in an emotional defense of personal or cultural assumptions about reincarnation—which may have been derived from respected religious sources—can be a waste of energy and even a waste of opportunity. We must be willing to entertain new perspectives. Our intuition must take wing. We need not fear the winds or fine air of spirit. In order to learn to fly, we cannot cling to the safe rocks of reasonable assumptions. Of course, we may wish to return to "ground." But, just as winged flight cannot cling to earth, higher thought cannot cling to reason—although knowledge of its topography may be a necessary aid for good navigation.

Those who wish to defend their assumptions and closely held concepts will discover little opportunity to do so in this work. A wise student must learn to withhold judgment and remain open to the guidance and intuition that come from higher realms. This involves learning to discriminate, discriminate, discriminate and let go of past assumptions.

Discrimination does not mean defending prejudice. Rather, it means intellectually distinguishing what is true. We must first open a channel of intuition and then, without assumptions, keep shifting intellectual and personal perspectives until our intuition makes a direct link with truth. We need to learn to trust this process and to trust that the truth will be revealed when we ask for help.

Prayer, in combination with right meditation and contemplation, remains the strongest human power on earth. We pray, therefore, for enlightenment and right guidance. We always recommend that sincere seekers strengthen and empower their meditations with direct prayer to God. Calling on a sacred name of God, such as Lord Christ, we pray to the angels of the Akashic Records for assistance. Such direct prayer always aids our attunement. I believe that this higher form of inner spiritual help is essential.

Understanding is quite difficult without some degree of personal identification with the story line. In fact, sometimes imagination is more important than knowledge. Does this seem strange? Meditate on it. It bears repeating: sometimes imagination is more important then knowledge!

Group Energy

The development of civilization has both a constructive and a destructive side. As conscious participants in a spiritual study of history, we must be conscious of, and aligned with, the constructive side—the healing of culture and society. Collective memory, as well as collective healing, is a group phenomenon. You can become a part of this group energy, even if anonymously. The more that any of us is able to do, the more powerfully our group effort will contribute to the collective well-being of society. As the energy of renewed understanding, vision and insight is made available, it will be easier for others to gain access, to share, to know.

The work we do now will help lighten the general atmosphere of the whole planet. This process has already begun to take place around us. For those who are aware of it, it is the very essence of the New Age. This small part of that greater work is not an effort that can be concluded in ten years; we are talking about centuries of work. It is helpful to remember, as we begin to do this work as consciously as we are able, that we can be internally supported by our group effort. The more strong-minded the individual student, the greater his or her influence on others.

In this type of effort, we can best help our spiritual brothers and sisters by working to expand—and correct—our own vision and grasp of history. Knowing who we are, where we have been and what we may have done in other lives is important. At the very least, this effort will help us recognize and support others who are following a similar earthly mission. It may help us, as well, to develop compassion for those who are still deceived by egoistic ambition, and who may have strayed down misguided roads.

Fame and Fortune

Fame is of a karmic nature. Most of us have never had a life that is known to history. However, having a famous life is neither good nor bad—except that those who have attained fame have a heavier burden to bear.

Ultimately, we are here to learn. The purpose of life is to grow strong spiritually. Learning the lessons of spirit—of service, self-sacrifice and obedience to the higher Spirit—is the true purpose of life. As living souls, we have entered the challenge of earth life in order to experience the power and responsibility of choice, creativity and personal will. Personal challenge is part of every life, no matter how evolved the soul.

Because we can learn by observing the struggles of others, we study past lives of famous people. The rich, famous and charismatic (what we call *highly karmic souls*) have, for the most part, simply taken on more responsibility. Personalities with worldly ambition pursue fame with great effort and desire. These are the actors, the great social performers of life. Such souls come to the forefront in almost all of their incarnations—called, it seems, by some collective memory of past deeds or by some more ancient karma.

In the arena of earth life, each soul moves with perfect mathematical precision and timing through the living consequences of his or her projected thoughts and desires. Every life is experienced in accordance with the principles of divine law. As one gives, so it is given unto that person. This is the rule of life. And it is affirmed by spiritual wisdom: "Do unto others as you would have them do unto you." "As you judge, so are you judged." "Judge not, therefore, and be not judged." "Love thy neighbor as thyself." These statements reflect the basic law of karmic consequence—the law of compensation.

Heroes, Myths and Archetypes

Some souls have long histories, going back millennia. Through glory after glory, triumph as well as failure, they marched across history, constantly drawn to action in karmic dramas. Whenever and wherever these strong ones incarnate, they tend to carve themselves a place in history. For better or for worse, these highly karmic souls leave large tracks in the permanent record of life on earth.

We need to become fully aware of the mythical basis to many of our hero legends. We must learn to discriminate between the hero-myth and the real-life drama. Tracking great cultural heroes through Akashic history is one way to gain access to the movement of groups through civilization. As former cultural heroes incarnate again, some karmic force seems to propel them to come forward and repeat the successes of former lives. This continues until something, usually a spiritual impulse, intercedes or transforms the karmic mandate.

If the Akashic researcher can identify them, these strong souls form what I call *road markers* within the Akashic Records. Such highly karmic and charismatic individuals often incarnate with a magnetic energy that is representative of their group. At least some, if not many, of the souls who previously incarnated with a particular leader are likely to reincarnate within the same karmic group.

The Burden of the Archetype

As one studies historical leaders who have had famous lives of powerful notoriety, one begins to wonder what is going on. How can one soul have so much karma? In regard to this, I refer to what I call the *burden of the archetype*, or the burden of a collective expectation.

For example, consider the question: was there a "Moses"? If there were a Moses, could the soul who played that part have been karmically influenced by the archetypal energy of a spiritual/moral leader—"the leader of God's people"?

Yes, such collective archetypes do exist. These archetypes originate from the accumulation of an ancient karmic energy that has a larger-than-life spiritual dimension. Alexander the Great is one example of a powerful highly karmic leader who assumed the burden of an archetypal energy (the perfect warrior). This soul has come to earth many times, recreating famous incarnations as a politician or warrior. The path of this "general of the East" has been toward Asia and Japan. I have noticed that whenever

Alexander has come back, many of his warriors reincarnate with him. In some cases, he has reincarnated with his army partially intact—a powerful example of group magnetism.

Some of these strong souls who are carriers of group karma take on the burden of an archetype. They can be profoundly affected by a sense of karmic obligation. Is it possible that the carrying of an archetype is, in itself, karmic? Why would anyone choose that archetype? It is as if they have demanded it, and have earned it as a karmic right. Perhaps the carrying of an archetypal energy is one of the products of worldly ambition. While many people have karma that makes them ambitious for fame in their present lives, bearers of an archetypal energy may carry a deeper karmic burden that originated in ancient times. For these souls, a rush to fame may come from a compulsion of which ambition is only the superficial expression.

Ancient orders of kingship that claimed god-on-earth status may have created deep karmic burdens that go beyond simple explanation. For example, Egyptian mummification magic and priest-craft rituals may continue to carry serious karmic repercussions. It is interesting to notice the multiple lifetime consequences of strong karmic bonding, such as that of Egyptian ritual magic, when observing past-life progressions. Former pharaohs and Egyptian royal-family members can become royalty once again according to their former lifetime expectations and even demands. As a principle, the rich tend to become richer, the poor (in discipline and expectation) tend to become poorer—depending on the karmic mind-set that such souls carry from life to life.

The Evolution of Archetypes

Present-day Western culture, with its Greco-Roman roots, is a mix of the history of Mesopotamian, Indo/Aryan and Egyptian civilizations. This mix includes the Persian/Zoroastrian religion, which preceded messianic Judaism and contributed to cultural blending. Later-day Zoroastrian messianic religion was a Puritan precursor to Judeo-Christian Pharaceeism—which, in turn, gave rise to the biblical assumptions of organized Christianity. This flow is not so complicated to see when approached through a methodical review of history.

With the acceptance of Christian-oriented Mithraism after the Council of Nicea, the Greco-Roman formation of the Church was partly complete. However, more was to come in the evolution of Christianity—the body of the Church continued to be reformed, becoming a house built not on the sands of human records, but on the eternal bedrock of spirit.

In the evolution of Western history, thousands of years of competing as well as complimentary cultures have flowed together, each slightly absorbing the culture before it. The new collective in each cycle retains what is desired or needed spiritually and culturally from prior civilizations. This adoption process always includes the esoteric, or spiritual, archetypes of the former cultures. The spiritual archetypes are mandatory. We, as a vast collective, carry these archetypes with us as part of the collective unconscious, a result of the collective psychospiritual progress of evolution through many ages.

The spiritual evolution of peoples and sub-groups is planetary in scope. In our studies, we will look at the formation of cradles of civilization, as well as the movement of soul cultures through time. As we contemplate the development of civilizations, and the continental zones occupied by those civilizations, we will consider the influence of what may be called *continental consciousness*.

Biblical Archetypes

Biblical history records the evolution of a "Moses" archetype; also a "King David" (spiritual leader) archetype and a "King Saul" (cultural leader) archetype. There is also an "Aaron" (priest brother of Moses) archetype and the archetype of "Joshua" (warrior leader). In addition, "God's people" is a strong universal archetype that is as ancient as the human social order, beginning much earlier than recorded biblical history.

Why are these archetypes given Judeo-Christian designations? Although the name for a given archetype can change with the times, for Western culture, these names have Judeo-Christian significance. Because the dominate culture in the West has been a by-product of Christian-based social history from the fourth century on, biblical archetypes have become a part of our collective reality. Whether the histories of famous lives, as described in the Old Testament, are factual or not, these roles have a powerful archetypal expression in the universal psychodrama of our collective history—perceived, amplified and sustained by collective expectation. Collective expectations generate karmic realities that, in turn, become an active part of collective history.

The "Moses" archetype goes back many thousands of years to regions that have little to do with Mesopotamia or with Hebrew mythology or fact. In other words, the "Moses" archetype is not an original Old Testament archetype. It became an Old Testament cultural motif with the creation of the original books of the Bible (between 770 and 220 B.C.).

Controversial Figures

Any approach to Akashic studies requires a universality of religious understanding, especially since some of our studies present insights into other lives of controversial figures. In fact, many lives of famous people who were involved in religious controversy can be identified in the Akashic Records. Past-life insights can inform us about the karmic and spiritual path of these individuals.

Although these types of cases can raise sensitive issues for people from some cultures or religious groups, I prefer not to avoid them. Rather, I would stress that we only have access to part of the karmic picture. The souls of these controversial individuals may have purposes and debts about which we know nothing. This world is filled with diversity—with different cultures, languages, religions and ethnic populations—all with different karmic needs. We must be open-minded and approach religion as we would approach the study of any culture or language.

The Timeline of History

Some people believe that the timeline of history can go in many directions. They think we can have multiple lifetimes without the common thread of past, present or future. These people consider the study of past lives to be more or less irrelevant since, with multiple simultaneous lives, there is no continuity from one life to the next.

Scientific inquiry has demonstrated a uni-directional, positive timeline in the physical realm—in biology, geology, chemistry and physics—at both the micro- and macro-levels of reality. Higher metaphysical principles also indicate a positive, uni-directional timeline with respect to physical incarnations. From a spiritual perspective, each life is better, or more progressed, than the ones that went before. Life is not about acquiring power or popularity; it is about a process of spiritual evolution—the paying of debts, learning soul lessons and, generally speaking, growing spiritually.

Once a life has been lived, it is permanently recorded as having been accomplished in the physical world. It can not be changed, negated or reversed. Therefore, the premise that there are multiple, simultaneous incarnations can be understood as evidence that astral events are taking place in realms that are not of the earth.

In these astral, or mental, realms, people can live out all possible scenarios. Some individuals may have many plays, many scripts, that are played out simultaneously. A play, or "rehearsal," on the astral plane can appear to some people as though it were an actual life-occurrence. However, such experiences have little effect on the progression of physical incarnations, except perhaps as tools to engage a fuller emotional experience, or to prepare the individual to participate more positively in the next life.

Whenever an individual's next incarnation does take place on earth, that earth-life becomes a fact—a real link in the progression of lives that preceded, and will follow, it. And it is so revealed in the Akashic Records. Because the physical plane timeline only progresses forward, when a physical incarnation occurs and a life becomes a fact, for better or for worse, all simultaneous astral possibilities with which that soul may have been playing no longer have any reality in earth history. Other possibilities can be played out on the astral level between lives, or even as active emotional imagination, but such a play does not appear in the Akashic Records as a true happening on the plane of history.

The lower astral realm is sometimes called the "Hollywood" of the heart, where artful dramas of fiction and imagination are played out. We must learn to intuitively recognize visions of astral realities, without confusing alternative inner levels of non-earth reality with historically founded planetary fact.

Soulmates

Our soul has two simultaneous aspects: a male polarity and a female polarity. Both can be in physical incarnation at the same time. This can lead to simultaneous or overlapping lives incarnating in two different locations—a phenomenon that can be difficult to interpret and that can create the mistaken impression that we do have simultaneous incarnations.

The simultaneous incarnation of the masculine and feminine parts of the soul has led some seers or sensitives to the type of interpretations that are found in romance novels about soulmates. The romanticism of a soulmate story is often highly idealistic. It is not always good for us to meet our soul half on the physical plane. In fact, meeting our soul half on the physical plane can be difficult to the point of karmic harm to the higher Self. Nevertheless, the principle of soul compliments, as expressed in the myth of Adam and Eve, is a valid and powerful transcultural archetype. Perhaps, eventually, when the vibrations of emotional passion are less destructive on earth, the meeting and happy marriage of true soulmates will become commonplace, rather than the exception.

From a less idealistic standpoint, an earthly soulmate does not have to be our exact other half. A soulmate can also be anyone from within our soul group.[2] When we have established a close intimate relationship with another male, or female, from our soul group, the other can reincarnate with us as what appears to be a soulmate. Such soulmates may or may not be lifelong partners; they may also be friends, brothers, sisters, mothers, fathers, fellow monks or nuns, comrades in a common cause, even co-workers during a particular life-cycle.

Occasionally, a soul will incarnate both masculine and feminine polarities in two same-polarity bodies—as both male or as both female. This can involve polarity reversal, such as a female born in a male body. As a general rule, the polarity stays with its body type or gender, and a gender reversal occurs only rarely—perhaps for the purpose of karmic correction. The two personalities may live in the same cultural area knowing one another as close friends, or they may not. Sometimes, the two parts of the soul incarnate on opposite sides of the world and have simultaneous, time-linked incarnations in entirely different cultures. The causal consciousness within the higher Self records these two different incarnations and absorbs the experiences of both at the same time.

Spiritual Initiation

In preparation for deeper understanding, it is necessary for students of Akashic history to seek out more information on the principle of inner spiritual evolution that is expressed through the process of initiation. This topic is more thoroughly covered in our inquiry into the lives of some former leaders of the theosophical movement.[3]

In human evolution, many lifetimes are spent developing basic survival skills and understanding. Although spiritual awareness is, and has always been, available from the higher realms,

---

[2] A soul group is a group of spiritual selves progressing closely together, like a spiritual family.

[3] It was the Theosophical Society that first popularized, in the nineteenth century, many such teachings of esoteric truth.

human beings at the earth-bound level have taken a long time to achieve greater spiritual awareness. Enlightenment comes with degrees of soul initiation.

Spiritual initiation indicates that a permanent step in soul growth has occurred. This is an inner-plane soul dynamic that can be expressed outwardly as spiritual influence or spiritual power in the personality. The terms *initiate* and *initiation* have been used, for example, in theosophical literature by Helena Blavatsky, to convey both an esoteric and an exoteric meaning. Sometimes the higher spiritual steps of conscious development (i.e., esoteric meaning) are inferred. But, more often, the meaning is limited to membership in an "informational elite." In this exoteric sense, one is referred to as an "initiate" if one has been given, or introduced to, secret knowledge.

True initiation, however, is not measured by such limited knowledge. From an esoteric perspective, spiritual initiation is more like ordination, or anointing, of the soul. It is an inner awakening and empowerment that occurs on the inner planes and radiates into the human life and persona. A true initiate is one who has achieved, or received, one or more of these great initiations. Between lives, the soul of an initiate continues to be identified by this designation. However, in each earth life, the initiate must re-experience the trials of awakening before that person can be considered a full spiritual initiate. Many lifetimes can be spent in preparation for initiation; one who is undergoing such preparation is referred to as a "probationer" on the path.

The Great Initiations

Five great initiations belong to the process of human evolution and lead to spiritual mastery. Each represents a step that is greater than the one before, and each takes many lifetimes of preparation and service to achieve. Such initiations are not achieved in a vacuum, but are always accompanied by higher beings, great angels or a master.

1. The first great initiation is often expressed as enlightenment of the will and brings permanent spiritual ennoblement. It can be a spiritualizing empowerment of the whole person, emphasizing

great courage of conviction, commitment to the divine spirit and willingness to serve a spiritual mission.

2. The second great initiation is enlightenment of the mind. It involves development of spiritual intuition, and empowers the initiate through love of God and love of the truth. A second-degree initiate tends to focus on the exercise of mental and intuitional powers. Such initiates are often the teachers of humanity and must confront problems of faulty collective ideation that can block or mislead the collective's progress. A second-degree initiate must shine as a light of truth to lead humanity out of the fog of intellectual sophistry.

3. The third great initiation involves direct communion between the inner spirit and mind and the causal world—the world of higher soul consciousness. With the third initiation, commonly called "sainthood," the emotions are purified and the person becomes more deeply committed to, and lives in service to, the divine plan. From the third degree onward, a soul has completed earth evolution and is no longer required to return. A third-degree initiate on the path of true inner light would only reenter an earth incarnation as a *Bodhisattva*, a saintly wayshower or pathfinder—a God-ensouled emissary on a mission to humanity.

4. The fourth great initiation is called the "great soul," or *arhat*, initiation. A fourth-degree initiate must take on the burdens of humanity and suffer the trials and challenges that this karmic path requires. These are the rare great souls who are chosen to incarnate after it is no longer required by karmic law. They have accepted the spiritual sacrifice of leading humanity forward by transforming collective conditions through their own personal lives.

Several of our case studies present the progression of such great souls. For example, the passion play of the crucifixion of Jesus expresses the fulfillment of this mystery, which concludes in the resurrection and ascension to full spiritual mastery.

5. The fifth great initiation is spiritual mastery. This initiation blends the former human into a superhuman being. A spiritual master is called a "full solar initiate." This degree of initiation is

the final human evolutionary step for the perfected Son of man. This is what all the higher mystical traditions, both East and West, have taught.

Achievement of spiritual mastery is a birth into higher causal reality. This final earth initiation occurs according to a timing that cannot be measured or reasoned out from facts of life as we perceive them. The soul within develops strength in God's own time.

Many of the conditions of spiritual consciousness described for the great initiations can be present, in part, in initiates at any stage, or even in a non-initiate. It is possible for an intellectual genius to have little or no spiritual enlightenment, yet to imitate greatness. This is not bad; it is part of the evolutionary process. Human beings imitate what they like, or desire to achieve. Some forms of enlightenment, especially the higher internalized states of cosmic consciousness, can occur spontaneously or can be stimulated through yogic practices. Such experiences are preparatory to a higher, more permanent spiritual awakening, but are not always the same as initiations.

The Way of The Saint

In human life, we must cultivate four things: love of God, a desire to be of service, an open mind and a willingness to learn. Learning the right use of creative energy, and its consequences, is probably the most important thing a soul must learn on earth. When this lesson has been learned, and karmic debts have been discharged, the cycle of reincarnation may be ended. A soul whose maturity and service are complete is free to pursue a life in the higher worlds of divine creation—realms of glory and beauty beyond anything known on earth.

Angelic Lines of Evolution

More than one line of evolution exists on earth. Closely connected to the human kingdom are the lower kingdoms—animal, mineral and vegetable. In addition, there is the angelic, *devic* or nature kingdom, that does not belong to the physical realm, and that includes beings who serve God and nature on the etheric plane. At the higher stages of their evolution, which progresses much more slowly than does human evolution, devic beings can develop great mental powers. Eventually, devic beings can evolve into angels.

Although few angels incarnate on the physical earth, beings from the higher devic line occasionally take human incarnations. It is difficult to tell if these devas are lost, accidentally trapped or simply sent by God.[4] In fact, human incarnations can be dangerous for even the most mature devas. This is because, while humans must deal with evil and darkness—often expressed as ignorant and selfish emotions—during the course of their physical incarnations, evil is something foreign or transient in the devic and angelic worlds. Because they have never experienced evil motivations within themselves, such beings can become lost when they enter a human incarnation.

The higher devic soul entering a human incarnation often possesses special gifts of genius. Some of earth's greatest artists and musicians have been physically incarnated higher devas. However, due to their inexperience with earth conditions and the strangeness of human emotions, such devas often struggle with emotional immaturity. Because it is difficult for them to express basic human emotions, these devas have a tendency toward eccentricity. Unaccustomed to the dynamics and pressures of the physical world, they may also express an excessive degree of self-centeredness. They may flee into their creative worlds as a means

----

[4] For more information on this subject, we refer you to *Angels of Nature*, by Dr. Stephen Isaac, or *Kingdom of the Gods* and *Fairies at Work and at Play*, by Geoffrey Hodson.

of escape, or reject human life altogether and crash into a world of sorrow or madness.

Those whom we designate as true angels are, in spirit, great beings who have evolved on the slower evolutionary path of nature's higher worlds. Such ones are exceedingly rare. An angel who incarnates physically for the first time is equivalent to a third-degree initiate, but has achieved this great level of spiritual development outside a physical incarnation.

We in the human community are often attracted to, or inspired by, those who come to us from the nature line of evolution. In their higher development, devas can reveal great spiritual powers. Their powers of spiritual magnetism call out to us, and their sensitivity and talents, which are often detached from human concerns, fascinate and charm us.

In some cases, the inner powers of these souls are expressed only through the mind or through an isolated aspect of development, such as the emotional power needed for poetry or music. Wolfgang Amadeus Mozart, for example, was a soul from the nature line of evolution. Such devic or angelic geniuses are not initiates in the human sense; they come among us to "earn their wings" under human conditions, for a mutual good.

Angels or highly evolved devas who dare to enter the human condition often express special qualities of intuition. Although these souls seem unusually close to the spirit, they sometimes seem strangely out of place, stumbling over even the most simple human choices. Unless they are able to learn quickly about the human condition, these beings are in danger of tripping over the lack of human experience within their personality.

The Study Premise

The following case histories of past lives of famous people are to be used for historical research. You are advised to meditate on one biography at a time, until a clear understanding of the interrelationship of lives can be grasped. Anyone doing past-life research will benefit from returning to the history books.

I recommend that anyone interested in Akashic history physically visit a library rather than just review biographical books from an armchair at home. This activity prepares our inner person to follow the same procedures during the hours of sleep, while attending a hall of learning in a higher dimension of consciousness.

In your historical research, follow these steps:

1. Review biographical material from various sources so that you can integrate different perspectives, religious views, secular views and so on.

2. Study both favorable and unfavorable biographies, particularly on lesser-known historical figures. In other words, do not be trapped by studying only biased views. If needed, obtain material with a foreign cultural perspective, perhaps originally written in a different language. Seeing different sides of an historical issue or event will help you recognize, avoid and overcome sociopolitical distortions and historical misinterpretations.

3. Meditate on those elements of personal character that demonstrate the consistent aspects of that person's individuality. Do not be afraid to question the assumptions of others, especially concerning established beliefs.

4. Demand the truth inwardly. Develop your own intuition. At the highest soul level, penetrate the inner realms of reality. Never give up! And accept no assumptions. To discover truth is the prime directive of pure science and philosophy. It is also the prime directive of every great religious faith. Truth is the guide we must remember as we view the complex maze of past and present memory that we call *Akashia*.

At the highest level of your intuition, you already have access to the inner records. However, in most cases, awakening higher levels of spiritual awareness in outer consciousness is a lifelong work. It may even be the work of many lifetimes. The case studies that follow constitute an exercise in this great work.

Let us now begin with the lives.

Acknowledgment

I wish to give special thanks to our sketch artist, Allison Ohman for her fine intuitive—and interpretive—pencil drawings. Base art for use in the studies was collected from many different sources, including ancient statues and frescos. From these miscellaneous images, some of which are well-known, Allison made quick, free-hand sketches using her eye and intuition in a way that carries a special touch. We feel that she has given a fine gift to this work and appreciate her continuing openness and help.

The Lives

48

Dante Alighieri
Poet in the East and the West

Lives of famous warriors and kings were probably the first individual lives recorded in human history. However lives of spiritual and literary artisans are often more interesting. Let us begin our studies with a Greek poet who lived five centuries before the time of Christ.

Pindaros
(522—443 B.C.)

Pindar was a Greek lyric poet who was born near ancient Thebes, in Greece. He composed numerous works, including some fine examples of early Greek literary poetry celebrating the gods, goddesses, victories in the national games, festivals and so on. *Pindar* wrote in support of aristocratic idealism.

He is famous, in part, because his life and works have been studied and commented upon by many hundreds, even thousands, of scholars from the fifth century B.C. to the modern day. Several famous writers of Greek and Roman antiquity, some considered fathers of Western philosophy and poetry, made flattering and exalted references to Pindar. With so much public homage to the high quality of his wordsmithing genius, *Pindar* was elevated to almost god-like status.

He has lived five public lives since the life of *Pindar*, four of which were quite famous. The fifth and last incarnation, as an

Englishman, was less famous but its connection to the other lives is nevertheless important. *Pindar* is an example of a soul who has functioned more in the realm of genius than in the human realm.

Pindar falls into the class of incarnated devic beings. Through several major incarnations, this wandering soul expressed a type of genius that has kept him somewhat out-of-balance. As a devic individual, he has had many difficult, seemingly self-destructive lives, yet he repeatedly contributed to cultural literature. He seems to have gotten stuck on the karmic wheel of life here on earth. Here is his progress after *Pindar*:

This same soul incarnated in China in the eighth century as *Li Po*, the Tang dynasty poet. *Li Po* was famous for his exquisite imagery, richness of language and cadence of lyrics. *Li Po* is said to have drowned by falling out of a boat while trying to embrace the moon reflected in the lake. This may have been a reference to depression that culminated in suicide. Alcohol, along with emotional sensitivity, played a part in that tragedy.

Li Po, Li T'ai-po
(700—762 A.D.)

Dante Alighieri
(June 5, 1265—Sept. 14, 1321)

Li Po returned to the West, incarnating in Italy in the twelfth century as the famous poet *Dante Alighieri*.

Who, in Western literary studies, is not familiar with the Renaissance poet *Dante Alighieri*? An Italian poet, born in Florence and entrusted with various diplomatic missions, he is the author of *The Divine Comedy*.

Dante, in his genius, was very free in his creation of theological illusions. He was so free that he became carried away—drunk on imagination, in a sense. He created imagery of the power of hell and the power of heaven. In *The Divine Comedy*, he described his visit to the lowest regions of the scorching, fiery hell, where he met a local magistrate and other historical people, whom he considered his political or social enemies. This could be seen as a form of irresponsibility; or was it literary license? Such literary license, however, carries karmic consequences.

Alexander Pope
(May 21, 1688—May 30, 1744)

51

We see this soul incarnating again in the West as *Alexander Pope*, British poet and satirist, author of the famous *Essay on Man*. *Pope* was, it is said, a primary literary force in the creation of modern English. He used language in an unusual way, impressing the world of his time with an innovative style of writing that evoked powerful images. *Dante Alighieri* was likewise famous for his contributions to modern Italian.

A common thread that runs through these four lives (*Alexander Pope, Dante Alighieri, Li Po* and *Pindar*) is that of profound ability as a wordsmith, creator and innovator of language. This devic soul has become magnetized karmically on the earth plane through fascination with the power of the written word. His particular genius is that of bringing new language into use.

Has this soul bound himself into karmic human circumstances through the magic and power of the written word? No matter how lofty a genius, if such a one is not able to get his feet squarely on the spiritual path, he can be bound by the magnetism of previous lives and by the force of the very things he wrote about. Creative choices made on the earth plane can develop along both constructive and destructive lines. The powers of light and of darkness express in terms of blessings or curses to create powerful karmic responses. Even the lives of more evolved souls can turn wayward, in a karmic sense, if these energies are misused. Along these lines, *Dante*'s satirical writings can be considered karmically irresponsible and potentially self-destructive.

The next life of this soul, who as *Alexander Pope* died in 1744, was a fairly rapid reincarnation as *Edgar Allan Poe,* the famous Boston-born American poet and author. This next life is an example of wayward creativity resulting in a lost-sheep type of spiritual illness, expressed as mental depression and emotional alienation. This karmic curve reaches back to the life of *Li Po*, as well. There is a certain sadness in this progression.

52

Edgar Allan Poe
(Jan. 19, 1809—Oct. 7, 1849)

Edgar Allan Poe is the author of *The Raven*, *Annabelle Lee*, and other well-known poems. He was also a social and political activist who, as in his other incarnations, became very much a man of his times, involved in the simultaneous pursuit of both his political ideals and literary genius.

Considering the progression of these five lives, this soul's progress seems more of a descent than an ascent. Each personality was driven further into the karmic consequences of the earth plane than was the previous incarnation. It is as if *Pindar* became more and more trapped by karmic consequences.

Edgar Allan Poe supposedly died from alcohol poisoning about two years after his first wife's death. At that time, he was engaged to be remarried. On the way to this wedding, he stopped at a tavern and became horribly drunk. He died a few days later. This is a karmic repetition that relates back to the Chinese poet *Li Po*, who drowned accidentally while intoxicated with alcohol.

Edgar Allan Poe was a sensitive person whose talent lay in the realm of imagination, and whose difficulty lay in the development of emotional expression. Such individuals can easily be trapped by addiction, seeking release in drugs and alcohol. Alcohol is especially dangerous for a temperamental deva, or nature being, who already has an inner drive to seek release from this world.

The length of time between lives for a soul with a high level of genius is normally two hundred years or more. Forty to a hundred years, on the other hand, is normal for the average human. More mature souls rarely come back in as short a time as forty years. However, quick re-embodiment is possible—even for older souls—under special circumstances, such as a life that has ended abruptly through violent death, suicide or accident. A quick return is especially likely if the death of the personality happened while the soul was still young and intensely involved in life plans.

The next incarnation of the devic *Pindar/Poe* was as the British writer *Allen Upward,* who was born in England in approximately 1895, and died in approximately 1925. He published an interesting book called *The Divine Mystery.* Another of his writings was the *Sayings of the Master Kung*, commentaries on the sayings of Confucius. In his introduction to *The Divine Mystery,*

Upward identified himself as a *changeling*, a term that refers to the deva.

In writing *The Divine Mystery, Upward* offended many important people in the publishing world of his time. As a result, he was rejected by the British elitist establishment. As a professional journalist with an anti-establishment attitude, *Upward* found employment difficult. He is practically unknown in modern literature, and his work is hard to find.

In *The Divine Mystery*, *Upward* discussed the development of the sacred word as a principle. According to *Upward*, three people became the collective literary (archetypal) Jesus of the Bible. These were Jesus of Nazareth, John the Baptist and another, also called Jesus, who was a founder of the Essene movement, about a hundred and sixty years before the life of Jesus of Nazareth. This thesis is intriguing and communicates an intuitive perspective of some importance.

Whom did *Allen Upward* offend? He offended all of British society, with the exception of perhaps a few theosophists. He offended orthodox Judaism, as well as Catholic society and the Church of England. In addition, he offended all established publishing interests, much to his own personal detriment. With his perverse sense of humor and pride, he actually seems to have tried to be offensive. Nevertheless, an honest scholar might argue that *Upward* was doing a fine job of putting the pursuit of intellectual truth before personal or cultural concerns. Any student of Akashic history should make an attempt to find and read *The Divine Mystery*.

As *Dante,* this soul used literary license to describe the descent into hell. Later, as *Poe*, his own karmic thought-energy drew him into a fascination with the dark side, inspiring him to write poetry that touched darkness through melancholic emptiness and images of fear. As *Upward*, this soul continued to pursue *Dante's* allegory of an ascent toward paradise, in search of enlightenment through the written word. *Upward's* short life represented a leap *upward* after the negative tone of *Edgar Alan Poe*. The pull of spirit reached out to redeem this devic wanderer. At some point, an angel of God may weigh the efforts of such a "stranger in a strange land" and, with a spirit of grace, help him find a way of return to his own land.

The story of this devic soul also reminds us of the allegory of Icarus in Greek myth, who flew too close to the sun on home-made wings, only to fall to his death on earth.

Goethe
Literary Genius

Our next study, that of the famous *Johann Wolfgang von Goethe,* is intended both to challenge assumptions and to led students to expand their understanding of progressions.

One of Germany's greatest literary figures, *Goethe* first studied law. His early writing, inspired by Shakespeare, fed the *Sturm and Drang* movement among German youth. While enthusiastically partaking of the pleasures of court life, *Goethe* simultaneously made exceptional contributions to his culture and time.

Johann Wolfgang von Goethe   *Hesiod*
(Aug. 28, 1749—March 22, 1832)   *(8th century B.C.)*

Goethe's work deeply touched many mystical and emotional strings, especially in the minds of those who shared his psycholinguistic collective. He possessed an uncanny skill at tapping the group unconscious. Many consider him to be one of the greatest literary masters of all time. We will follow this soul through four famous and interesting lives. Our study begins with one of the world's earliest accessible literary personalities, the Greek epic poet *Hesiod*, and continues with the Roman poet *Ovid*.

Hesiod a creative genius, was a devic soul like Pindar. He has been on earth longer than has Pindar, possessing less spiritual maturity, if not less genius. The primary subjects of *Hesiod's* writings were the epic myths of the gods, as well as social myths. *Hesiod* has another famous incarnation (with more than one incarnation between these famous lives) as the Roman *Ovid*.

Ovid Publius Ovidius Naso   *Hermann Hesse*
(March 20, 43 B.C.—18 A.D.)   *(July 2, 1877—Aug. 9, 1962)*

Publius Ovidius Naso, known as *Ovid*, was a Latin lawyer-turned-poet who wrote his verse while in exile on the Black Sea. This incarnation reflected an undeveloped emotional life. Best-known for his book *Metamorphosis*, *Ovid* wrote in a simple, fluid manner about erotic and mythological themes. This soul (with other lives in-between) incarnated in Germany in 1749 as our even more famous subject, *Johann Wolfgang von Goethe*. The soul of *Goethe* reincarnated again fairly quickly to become the well-known German/Swiss author *Hermann Hesse*.

57

Hermann Hesse wrote *Siddhartha*, *Magister Ludi*, and *Steppenwolf*, among other important works. The son of missionaries to India, his books deal with the consequences of spiritual loneliness.

In the life as *Hesse*, this soul embraced humility in a way that began to heal his self-pride. You are advised to take this study (*Hesiod, Ovid, Goethe* and *Hesse*) and work deeply with these lives in meditation. Study the biographies with an understanding that these personalities belong to the same soul. You may also wish to compare the thought images and karmic energies in *Goethe's* novel *Die Leiden des jungen Werthers* with *Hesse's* personal difficulties with melancholia.

A recipient of the Nobel Prize for literature in 1946, *Hesse's* life represented a struggle and search for personal spiritual breakthrough. His writing is a good example of literary channeling, in which a great poetic genius defined the public need for collective spiritual awakening.

Paracelsus
The Healing Master

Our next study includes two very special elder souls, both literary geniuses working their way along the path of spiritual initiation. Spiritual mastery is exceedingly rare on the earth plane. The two great ones we will discuss (one from the human line and the other from the angelic line) are now initiates of the fifth degree—spiritual masters. As was mentioned in the introduction, spiritual mastery is not something achieved through earth lives alone, but rather is the result of an inner soul unfoldment on the higher planes of being.[5]

In their last human lives, these two elder souls were both fourth-degree initiates, called *arhats* (great souls). The first of the two had a famous life as *James the Less* the biblical brother of Jesus.

James the Less, Essene Brother of Jesus of Nazareth
(d. 1st century A.D.)

James the Less, also referred to as *James the Righteous*, was the half-brother of Jesus, a son of Joseph from an earlier marriage. He was the author of the letter of *James* in the New Testa-

---

[5] It is recommended that you read available theosophical material on this subject, for example, C. W. Leadbeater's *The Masters and the Path*, which provides a good basic introduction to the concept of inner growth through spiritual initiation. Also recommended is Alice Bailey's *Initiations, Human and Solar*.

ment. Older than Jesus, James was a leader in the Essene community in Jerusalem.

An eclectic group of Hebrews, Aramaics, Greeks and Syrians, the Essenes were evangelistic protestants who were agents of change for their time and culture. In addition to their monastic order known as the *desert fathers*, the Essenes were organized as a social community that included both male and female members in a family congregation. The social Essenes later reincarnated in the West through such movements as the Waldensees, the German Quietists and the English Quakers.

In their early years, both *James* and Jesus were followers of John the Baptist. After the death of John, Jesus became the recognized leader of the movement; after the death of Jesus, *James the Less* was recognized as the leader. The Essenes called themselves "Followers of the Way," "Followers of the Way of Righteousness" and "Doers of the Law." The root word that we have interpreted as *Essene* most likely had an Aramaic root relating to "doers" or "followers" of the path of righteousness.

James The Less was an arhat, a fourth-degree initiate. He was one of the most advanced souls in incarnation at that time, besides John the Baptist and Jesus. *James* was, in his own right, a messiah according to the traditional Hebrew meaning of the term: "a servant sent, or anointed, by God." Jesus and John the Baptist were also messiahs; in addition, Jesus was a fully developed spiritual master—the master, indeed, of both *James the Less* and John.

James walked firmly on the path of human evolution. He had three additional famous lives before he concluded his ascent to spiritual mastery—following his last life in the twentieth century. In his next famous life, the soul of *James the Less* incarnated in Switzerland in the sixteenth century as the enigmatic healing adept *Theophrastus Bombastus von Hohenheim*, who was called *Paracelsus*—an arhat, a fourth-degree initiate and a great soul way-shower.

Incarnating in Europe at the time of the late Renaissance, *Paracelsus* became a physician and alchemist and author of numerous medical and esoteric works. His previous lives included many as a strong and wise teacher; as a priest in Egypt, Chaldea and Babylon and, several times, as a healer in China. He also incarnated several times as a healer and yogi in India. His incarnation as *James the Less* occurred between two lives in India, just before he became Paracelsus. In his last life on earth prior to achieving mastery, this great soul was the Swiss poet and philosopher *Henri Frederic Amiel*.

Paracelsus
(1493—1541)

Henri Frederic Amiel
(1821—1881)

Henri Amiel was the author of the introspective diary that is sometimes called *Amiel's Journal*, or *A Journal In Time*. Through *Amiel's* diary, we can discern the genuine benevolence and beauty of this true spiritual genius. This soul's last life was magnificently humane, but also somewhat ordinary. Humility of mind and temperament was his last testament.

A careful comparison of the lives, writings and consciousness of *Paracelsus* and *Amiel*, who lived three hundred years apart, will amaze any scholarly minded and discriminating researcher. The psychic energy of *Amiel* is also similar to that of *James the Less* and his master, Jesus. In fact, this soul-energy signature has confused some Akashic readers who have incorrectly reported that Jesus incarnated as a healing master in India after his life in Palestine. Such readers were mistakenly tracking the soul who had been *James the Less*.

The great soul who was *James the Less*, having received the initiation of spiritual mastery, now works in full consciousness in the hierarchy of perfected souls for the ongoing healing and upliftment of humanity. He has become a "pillar" of God's kingdom, in the biblical sense, which means "to go out no more." Those who give this study due diligence will see the connections between these lives.

Kahlil Gibran
An Angel in Incarnation

Our next study covers other lives of *Kahlil Gibran*, an incarnating angel. This is the history of a very special pathfinder mission, and one of the most unusual life studies found in the Akashic Records. Taking on the sheath of mortality, with all its pains and trials, this angel continued to brave the elements of human incarnations until he achieved spiritual mastery.[6]

We first find this soul in the life of a writer who was an angel incarnate. In that life, which may have been his first in the human line of evolution, he was an inspired, prophetic playwright of religious passion, named *Elias*.

Elias of Hebron
(c. 260 B.C.—160 B.C.)

Elias lived approximately two hundred years before *John the Baptist*. His literary contribution, *The Book of Daniel*, was a great work of religious inspiration that expressed the coming changes of the ages. The story of Daniel is an exceptionally fine example of religious channeling. It expresses many strong thought-forms and allusions, such as those in Daniel's dream. Daniel dreams that his head is on the bed of the king. Is it not interesting that, in

---

[6] In the realm of angels this degree is equivalent to archangel.

his later life as *John the Baptist, John* loses his head to King Herod Antipas? Is this an example of self-fulfilling prophecy? The power of karmic prophecy is at work in the relationship between the *Book of Daniel* and the life of *John the Baptist*.

As we have seen in the lives of Pindar and Goethe, great responsibility and karmic magnetism are generated by the written word. In the creative exercise of literary art, karmic substance is created by whatever is written; even fiction has the power to become reality in a karmic future. On some level, somewhere, someone may live it. This is especially true for writing that is undertaken as a sacred task. Since the angel soul of *John the Baptist* was a powerful creative genius, although his work was intended as religious inspiration, it became prophecy.

John the Baptist was a desert esthetic, a spiritual prophet in the same mode as many of the Old Testament desert fathers. *John* was also a reformer and visionary leader of the messianic Essene community. In the biblical story of *John the Baptist, John* was a herald of the coming kingdom of God. Without question, the "kingdom of God" was an Essene premise, for which Jesus subsequently took up the mantle of leadership, perfecting its principle and vision—a fact that has been mostly lost to history.

After *John* spoke out against Herod Antipas, king of Palestine, Herod had *John* arrested. Since he was interested in messianic religion and Essene kingdom-of-God beliefs, by keeping *John* in prison, Herod had the opportunity to spend time with him. In a strange and perverse way, the king had captured his own spiritual teacher. *John* was patient with his disciple, for the potential conversion of a king hung in the balance.

Parts of the story of Daniel in the *Book of Daniel* preview events in the life of *John the Baptist*, the great psychodrama in which *John* lost his head to King Herod Antipas. According to that story, Herodias, Herod's wife, convinced Salome, her daughter by Herod's brother, to dance for Herod. When Herod was drunk, Herodias, who was jealous of *John,* told Salome to ask Herod for a boon if she were to dance for him. The drunken Herod said, "I will give you anything you want." Salome then asked for the head of *John the Baptist*. Since the request was made in the presence of guests, and the king was embarrassed to go back on his word, he turned to one of his guards and said, "Make it so." And so *John* lost his head.

Although we can conclude that *Elias* wrote his own future story line, this entire process can, nevertheless, be said to reflect the "will of God." When a prophet becomes an instrument of true prophecy, is that not the work of God? The honorable way that the angel of prophecy, Gabriel, is mentioned in the *Book of Daniel* is a hint of the higher reality that continues to work in each of the lives of this angel soul.

The coming Christ passion play required the death of *John the Baptist* so that his followers could begin to rely on Jesus as their leader. This brought Jesus, who was a spiritual master, to the forefront. The death of *John* set the stage for the great "Messiah advent." Through the Christ passion play, we observe the creation of a new pattern of service and expression for the planetary Christ. This, in turn introduced a new spiritual paradigm of thought and emotion and a new standard for spiritual initiation for the next twenty-six-thousand-year grand galactic cycle for humanity. From the *Book of Daniel* we read: "He said, 'Go your way, Daniel, for the words are shut up and sealed until the time of the end...go your way until the end; and you shall rest, and shall stand in your allotted place at the end of the days.'"

65

This soul incarnated again to perform an important service of religious inspiration in the crumbling Roman world of the sixth century, under circumstances that were made difficult by social ignorance, confusion and fear. He incarnated again as *St. Benedict of Nursia*, founder of the Benedictine order and father of European monasticism. In this, we find a direct karmic link to the tradition of the Essene fathers.

Benedict of Nursia, *St. Benedict*, whose given name was originally *John*, lived for many years in a cave. His story is similar to that of *John the Baptist*. When he emerged from his meditation and lengthy stay in the cave, this hermit denounced the worldliness and social disorder of his time. He let it be known that he would henceforth be called *Benedict* and that he would continue in a spiritual life.

The name *Benedict* comes from a verse in the Bible called the "Benedictus," or the "Song of Zachariah," which includes the invocation "Even so, Lord, come." This is the verse known as the traditional invocation of the "Coming of the Lord." Recall that Zachariah was also the father of *John the Baptist*, who was recorded in the Bible as having used those words in submission to a vision brought by an angel. The chosen name *Benedict* thus connects to Zachariah and to the life of *John the Baptist*.

John of Nursia, St. Benedict   *John Bunyan*
(c. 480 B.C.—543 B.C.)   *(1628—August 31, 1688)*

As we study the founding of the Benedictine order and see how much religious and educational work was done by its monks, it is not difficult to realize what a profound leader this great soul was. The spiritual needs of the sixth century were acute, and freedom of religion was expressed only through submission along narrow lines and in separation from society. The Benedictines designed a society for religious retreat and for survival—much as the Essenes had done.

The Benedictines represent a group reincarnation connected with the early Essene fathers of 200 B.C. In *St. Benedict*, we see that the former *John the Baptist*, who had been a desert hermit, had become more active in his participation in a social role. Bringing a personal love for art and literature into active expression,

Benedict encouraged his followers to do the same. This first of the Catholic religious orders helped rescue and preserve many precious items of art and literature during a time of social upheaval. In this way, the Benedictine monasteries became organized centers of culture, religion and education that, for all practical purposes, stabilized European culture during the crumbling of the Roman Empire.

This soul's next three incarnations came together fairly quickly. It is not ordinary for a soul who is so highly evolved to incarnate in lives close together—but this is no ordinary soul. He did what we can call a "one-two-three" of related incarnations on earth— one life after another for acceleration, like skipping a rock over the water. Each of these lives was a little bit more personal in its content, a little more focused and creative. The momentum was a movement toward completion.

In fulfilling mastery on earth, this great angel attained full knowledge of humanity. There can be no question about the fine genius in his soul. At the same time, each of his next three lives was progressively more human than the last—more loving, more humble, more accepting, less intense and fiery, less rigid in religiosity. Submission to God extinguished his spiritual pride. Humble acceptance of humanity, without capitulation to inertia, was a mark of this great soul.

67

In his next life, this soul became *John Bunyan*, an English preacher and writer. *John Bunyan* spent twelve years in prison for preaching without a license. It may be difficult for modern students of history to realize that it has not been that many years since public speaking or teaching about any religious content required an official license. This rule was almost universal in European feudal society.

In his former life as *John the Baptist*, this soul used the time in Herod's prison for what can be considered a good religious purpose—the potential conversion of the king. In yet another life, *St. Benedict* spent up to twelve years in a cave doing preparatory religious work. While in prison, *John Bunyan* wrote *Pilgrims Progress*, a religious allegory about moral right and wrong in a Christian context. It became the second most popular book in the

English-speaking world. For more than two hundred years, only the Bible was used more often as the primary tool in English-speaking elementary schools.[7]

In his next life, in an age of spiritual ascendancy of light over darkness, this soul became a creative genius who suffered frustration in both his personal and artistic lives. *William Blake* was a Renaissance man who bridged the old and the new in his art and writing.

William Blake   *Kahlil Gibran*
(Nov. 28, 1757—Augt. 12, 1827)   *(Jan. 6, 1883—April 12, 1931)*

A British artist, author, poet, social revolutionary and mystic, *William Blake* was an influential person in the liberal artistic community of his age in London. He wrote fine mystical poetry and also contributed drawings and etchings on religious themes.

Blake made his living as an artisan by developing copper plate etchings as a commercial art form. Interestingly, some of the earliest monastic writings from the Essene community, with which *John the Baptist* was associated, were also etched in copper. Roles of etched copper were found in the caves of Qumran as part of the collection of the Dead Sea Scrolls. Thus, we find a past-life link in *Blake's* work with copper etchings. In addition, *John Bunyan* was the son of a metal smith and received early training in metal work.

William Blake is an example of an angel who became a master through human incarnation. In fact, he is perhaps the only such

---

[7] The English world at that time represented a reincarnation of Roman patterns and energies from the third through the sixth centuries A.D.

example to date in all of human history. For this reason, studying *Blake's* persona in his time and society is quite interesting. This is a study that should be taken on in depth. For example, *Blake* was a friend of Thomas Paine, who became one of the important intellectual forces of the American Revolution and of democratic movements worldwide. *Blake* helped Paine, who himself was an arhat, to escape arrest in England, urging him to leave that country just in time. This can be interpreted as an intervention prophecy involving grace since, without Paine's contributions, the American republic might not have established the first government in the Christian world to mandate complete religious freedom. Thus the fine threads of history weave their patterns from age to age.

This soul incarnated once more on earth before the incandescent sun of spiritual mastery was lit in its soul forever. This last life was the most down-to-earth personality of this soul—a genius, yet more gentle and loving, more protective toward women and completely immersed in his own humanity. *William Blake* became *Kahlil Gibran.*

The last earth life of this soul was as the beloved poet, *Kahlil Gibran.* A Syrian Christian poet, painter and author of many books, *Gibran* was most famous in the West for *The Prophet,* a book of religious sayings in prose and poetic form. He was born in Lebanon, completing a circle of spiritual energy that began in the Middle East with the life of *John the Baptist.* His first prose work was written in Arabic. He later learned to write in English, and eventually lived in the United States. In the 1920s, *Gibran* was well-known in the art community of Greenwich village, in New York City.

69

Of these six lives in progression (*Elias, John the Baptist, John Benedict of Nursia, John Bunyan, William Blake* and *Kahlil Gibran*), the one who would have been the most gentle and easiest to talk with, the most interesting, least harried and strained and perhaps the most balanced human, was *Kahlil Gibran.* While the persona lives out a full creative life by participating in the passions and processes of its age, the soul—in a way that is hidden and ineffable—is weighed and measured by God. The coming of spiritual mastery is a complete transmutation of the lower self and a birth into immortality. Few are the masters, yet the spiritual power and cosmic influence of one is equivalent to that of all the saints combined, because they directly reflect the consciousness of higher Spirit.

The apparent phonetic correspondence between the name *Kahlil Gibran* and the angel Gabriel is important. We recommend that this phonetic coincidence be the subject of deep reflective meditation. The soul of *Gibran*, who worked through several human incarnations with the spiritual gift of prophecy, finally became an officiate of the archetypal "office" of the archangel Gabriel. As such, his spiritual duty was to form a bridge between the higher worlds and the lower planes of material life by providing the "word" of prophecy.

From the higher worlds, the archangel Gabriel was, for two thousand years, *Gibran's* spiritual mentor. Now that *Gibran's* soul has achieved full spiritual mastery, he himself will serve to shepherd human evolution. Thus, he who brought us *Daniel* twenty-two hundred years ago has finally achieved his "...allotted place at the end of the days," as prophesied by the archangel Gabriel in the *Book of Daniel*. For this great one, the karmic circle of prophecy is complete.

Churchill
Greece and Rome in the
Twentieth Century

We will now look at three related lives that can help us see how related communities evolve in karmic clusters. This study presents the lives of a soul who has been a very charismatic figure in history. These lives, which tie together three cultures, are the Roman orator, politician and literary talent, *Marcus Tullius Cicero*; the fourth century B.C. Greek mercenary adventurer, orator and historical writer *Xenophone* and the twentieth century British politician and historian, *Sir Winston Churchill*. After one has spent some time studying these lives and their related cultures, and meditating on the characteristics common to all three, it is not difficult to grasp the progression of these lives.

71

Xenophone
(c. 434—355 B.C.)

Xenophone was a Greek mercenary four centuries before Christ who, along with thousands of other Ionian soldiers, sold his military services to the Persian empire. In his early years in Athens, *Xenophone* was a pupil of Socrates, the Athenian moral philosopher and teacher, who—himself an arhat—was one of the guiding lights of Western civilization. In his writing,

Xenophone depicted Socrates as a common-place, middle-class philosopher.

According to some scholars, *Xenophone* competed with Plato and other Greek philosophers for attention as the superior moral voice of his time. No friend of democracy, he was a conservative defender of the old ways. One of his books elevated the Persian conqueror Cyrus the Great as an example of enlightened leadership. He was a friend of what he considered to be the "good" warlords, conquerors and tyrants, and envisioned a higher standard for enlightened dictatorship. He was a politician with a superiority complex.

Xenophone was most famous for accompanying 10,000 Greek mercenaries to Persia. As the story goes, the leaders of the military expedition were invited to dinner by the local Satrap and were all murdered. *Xenophone* delivered a rousing speech to the remaining leaderless mercenary force, counseling strength and courage. We know of his story by his own writing, which portrayed him as the hero. The story is called the *Anabasis*, or the *Retreat of the Ten Thousand*. On his return to Ionia, *Xenophone* joined the Spartan army and was banished from Athens, his home city.

It is not difficult to identify Persian, Spartan and Athenian karmic energies in the Roman world at the time of *Cicero*.

Marcus Tullius Cicero
(106—43 B.C.)

Time and time again, when beginning a study of the life of *Cicero*, students encounter quotes such as the following from

American historian John Lord, in 1883: "*Marcus Tullius Cicero* is one of the great lights of history because his genius and influence were directed to the conservation of what was most precious in civilization among the cultivated nations of antiquity."

While it is not our intent to take *Cicero* down from his high cultural pedestal, we must look carefully at such interpretations. Those who make statements like the one above are obviously projecting their own bias toward conservative antiquity—which, due to its dependence on slavery and social domination does not have much to recommend it to posterity. It is possible to appreciate history without making excuses for human greed and ambition. It remains a basic spiritual principle that those who do not hear the messages of spirit, and who cling to material excess and selfish ambition to the detriment of others, are hiding under a dangerous cloak of egotistical ignorance. Such was the cultural condition of Rome in the first century B.C. *Cicero* was a moralist with an understanding of immortality. He was a social prophet who argued against social excess. His light was bright, at least in contrast with the spiritual poverty of his time.

Cicero gained a high reputation, at least in part, because he was an avid student of history and culture, especially of classic Greek literature and philosophy. He was an accomplished orator who developed a new and refreshing use of language and who was able to merge this clear use of language in both his writing and speaking styles. *Cicero* was a hero of the Roman ideal who expressed the moral voice of his times. In fact, the literary persona he projected appeared to be a finer character than he most likely was in real life.

73

Cicero held a position in political and social commentary that defined a changing era. His role as a political in-fighter was considered irresistible by some admirers of Roman culture. His rise to the head of the Roman republican forum in its last days was phenomenal. He came from new wealth and moved forward in social position on his talent alone.

Cicero's charisma and public appeal, even his talent, can be traced to the influence, both conscious and unconscious, of *Xenophone's* writing on the intelligentsia of Rome. The *Anaba-*

sis of *Xenophone* was a universal educational tool for all Roman aristocratic youth by the first century B.C. *Cicero* rode on a wave of psychic energy that emanated from the public appeal of *Xenophone's* heroic triumphs. He carried the other life charm of a moral hero. This is how karma works.

Sir Winston Leonard Spencer Churchill
(Nov. 30, 1874—Jan. 24, 1965)

74

You are advised to read a concise biographical sketch of the life of *Sir Winston Churchill.* You will discover that it reads exactly as if *Cicero* had been reborn in England. If you study *Churchill's* life, you will find that it matches the cumulative lives of *Cicero* and *Xenophone* with amazing accuracy.

Perhaps even more important than a study of these particular lives is the comparison of British empire of the early twentieth century—with its aristocracy, political pride, military adventurism and colonial conquests—with the inner karmic energies of Rome, Sparta and Athens, as well as the even earlier Mesopotamian Indo-Aryan cultures of conquest.

Churchill was born in an aristocratic British family. Longing for adventure, the young man (avoiding academia) attended military school, then joined the army. He was captured in the Sudan during a military campaign of the Boer War and made a spectacular escape, quickly becoming a public celebrity. Like *Xenophone*, he had hero karma. The phenomenal fortune and influence of his life was compounded by the unconscious Roman memory of the British people.

Churchill was elected to Parliament in his twenties. He led his people in two wars, switching from one political party to another according to the advantage of the moment. He was a powerful speaker. During the darkest days of World War II, he gave the British people courage by speaking to them over the radio. "If *Churchill* is unbreakable, then England is unbreakable," was the popular saying.

Nevertheless, British politicians set *Churchill* aside when they did not need him any longer. He disliked being displaced from the circle of power, and drank a lot. This recalls the pitiful, complaining letters and self-depreciating emotional pathos expressed by *Cicero*, when he was expelled from Rome for a year after making the politically dangerous choice of supporting Pompey over Julius Caesar.[8]

Repetition compulsion was also active in *Churchill's* intellectual life. In his spare time, after he retired, he wrote the five volume *History of the English Speaking People*—a project *Xenophone* or *Cicero* would have attempted.[9]

[8] Pompey has since been a king in England in the twelfth century and incarnated in America in the twentieth. Julius Caesar had incarnated East into Asia and Japan and again in America in the twentieth century. *Churchill* met both the former Pompey and the former Julius Caesar during his life, but without political strife or animosity. Neither of these two former Roman leaders was active in twentieth century Europe.

[9] Notice the vague phonetic correspondence in names. Sound is one of the creative forces of the inner life and sometimes is reflected in karmic/spirit connections.

Plutarch

The Historian

Another example of the Greco-Roman/British connection can be found by comparing the British historian *Arnold Toynbee* with one of Western history's most famous moral essayists, *Plutarch.* The next study opens a window of understanding into the developing character of one who was a talented teacher of social ethics. While perhaps not a great soul in the spiritual sense, he was, nevertheless, a valuable contributor to his society, culture and the field of education.

Plutarch
(c.46—c.120 A.D.)

Arnold Joseph Toynbee
(Apr. 14, 1889—Oct. 22, 1975)

An important Greek writer of the early Roman period, *Plutarch* is primarily known for his collection of essays called *Plutarch's Lives*, studies of the parallel lives of famous Greek and Roman political and military leaders and cultural heroes. *Plutarch* was a positive contributor to his society, as a priest, politician and teacher. In early life, he traveled from his home near Chaeronea, in Boetia (near Delphi), to Athens and Egypt. Later in his life, in about 90 A.D., he traveled to Rome on public business as an elected emissary from his home city.

The *Parallel Lives* of *Plutarch,* a series of books from which *Plutarch's Lives* was extracted, has been a major teaching contribution to Greco-Roman/European culture for almost two thousand years. The karmic dynamic of this contribution cannot be underestimated. This soul, to whom we refer with loving, good humor as "Professor" *Plutarch,* could not incarnate anywhere in the Western world without carrying the karma of having contributed to the higher moral education of millions of souls.

Plutarch's philosophical views may have been influenced by the school known as *Eclectic,* that advocated adoption of universal religion, morality and culture. *Plutarch,* although himself a Greek, admired the qualities and achievements of the Romans and accepted the rule of Roman imperialism over Greece without question. This karmic attitude led to a later incarnation as a socially well-adjusted professor in British society.

Arnold Joseph Toynbee, the twentieth century British historian, is best known for his twelve volume *Study of History.* From 1919 to 1924, he was a professor of Byzantine and modern Greek languages, literature and history at the University of London. In 1919, at the end of World War I, *Toynbee* was a British delegate to the Paris Peace Conference. From 1925 to 1955, he continued at the University of London as professor of international history, as well as serving as director of studies at the Royal Institute of International Affairs.

Toynbee has been criticized by some of his contemporaries for being more of a moral/speculative philosopher than an historian. Embracing a more universal world view than his contemporaries, *Toynbee* argued that civilizations break down when a dominant minority stifles the freedom and creativity of other minorities. *Toynbee* foresaw a future in which the best of Western and Eastern traditions combined in a new, universal religion. In these beliefs, we see the influence of *Plutarch's* universalism and multiculturalism and perhaps even a remnant of the influence of *Plutarch's* eclecticism. Is there an unconscious attempt in *Toynbee's* writing to make up for *Plutarch's* seemingly passive acceptance of Roman imperialism? This is an interesting question to ponder.

Disraeli and Tutu
Balancing Cultural Karma

This next study compares the South African Anglican Church Archbishop, *Desmond Tutu* with the nineteenth century British politician and prime minister, *Benjamin Disraeli*. Because this study involves a person still living, we are reminded that this text should be considered a forum for spiritual and educational purpose only. For some, this presentation may seem racially shocking or culturally disrespectful. Patience and open-mindedness are recommended.

The value of presenting this particular past-life connection is evident from the karmic precision that it reveals. Serious students are urged to pursue their biographical review beyond a superficial study. Comparing *Disraeli's* involvement in colonial imperialism with the chosen life work of *Tutu* is a good stimulant to intuitive understanding of a karmic condition. Let your intuition do the work.

Benjamin Disraeli
(Dec. 21, 1804—Apr. 19, 1881)

Benjamin Disraeli was born into a Jewish/Christian family in London, his family having migrated to England from Italy in the mid-eighteenth century. Benjamin's father, Isaac D'Israeli, was a talented novelist of Jewish Italian heritage who converted the family to Christianity. This socio-religious conversion had a two-fold effect on the life of *Benjamin Disraeli*. First, an outsider stigma contributed to his social competitiveness, a desire to fit in—to be more British than the British, more elitist than the elitists, more conservative than the conservatives, more High Church Christian than the High Church Christians. Second, *Disraeli* spent his life seeking social approval and recognition. By the time he became a friend and personal confidant of Queen Victoria, he had reached the height of his ambition. No one in British society could fail to recognize his position of influence on the inside.

Disraeli, who, like his father, was a novelist, wrote about dreams and visions that delved into the religious issue of Jewish history fulfilled within Christianity. In his novels, *Coningsby* (1844) and *Sybil* (1845), *Disraeli* speculated on the failures of the modern church and state and dedicated his considerable talent to the expansion of the British empire and the betterment of the British people.

Disraeli's second ministry, from 1874 to 1880, is most notable for its aggressive foreign policy. This included annexation of the Fiji Islands in 1874, and the Transvaal in South Africa in 1877. The British went to war against the Zulu in 1879 in the Transvaal. This war aggravated karma antagonistic to the Dutch Africans and led, after *Disraeli's* time, to the British death camps of the Boer War of 1899.

79

We are reminded that the greatest danger in political karma is that it does not necessarily stop when the individual is no longer in incarnation. Another political incarnation as a consequence is more of the rule than the exception. The difficulty of incarnating as a consequence of political karma is that the new life may not succeed in correcting the problem. Instead, the soul can become involved in worsening the situation, thereby creating more karma. This is often how it works.

In 1876, in his old age, *Disraeli* encouraged Queen Victoria to assume the title of Empress of India. For him, this was the crowning accomplishment of a long career of loudly proclaiming British imperial interests. The queen, who greatly adored *Disraeli,* made him First Earl of Beaconsfield as a reward.

Archbishop Desmond Tutu
(Oct. 7, 1931—)

This soul's next incarnation followed quickly, bringing him into a black South African family. Ordained in the Anglican Church in 1960, The *Rt. Rev. Desmond Tutu* served as Anglican dean of Johannesburg from 1975 to 1976, and as bishop of Lesotho from 1976 to 1978. In 1979, he was made the first black general secretary of the South African Council of Churches, representing over twelve million Christians.

80

Tutu was appointed the first black bishop of Johannesburg in 1984, the same year that he received the Nobel Peace prize. In 1986, he was elected the first black Anglican archbishop of Cape Town. An international spokesman for black nationalism, *Archbishop Tutu* has continued to work tirelessly to end apartheid in South Africa. He has published two volumes of sermons and addresses: *Crying in the Wilderness* (1982) and *Hope and Suffering* (1983).

Anwar el Sadat
The Karmic Path of a Soldier Soul

Is there such a thing as a "soldier soul"? We will savor this question in the following study and allow an answer to present itself solely through intuition.

The karmic path of the one known to us as *Anwar el Sadat* flowed through four famous lives—as a soldier, political leader and tactician. The progressive direction of these four lives defined a circle of karmic return with roots in Egypt twenty-seven hundred years ago.

Psalmtic, Pharaoh of Egypt
(c. 700 B.C.)

In the history books, we can find some biographical material on the life of the Egyptian pharaoh called *Psalmtic*, or *Psalmeticus*, a revolutionary leader who restored Egypt to cultural autonomy after many years of repression and tribute-taking from Eastern invaders. Essentially, *Psalmtic* was a political tactician who served as an administrative vassal and executor over Egypt for a foreign power. Having made terms with the foreigners who were centered in Babylon at that time, *Psalmtic* waited until he could strengthen Egypt and mount a successful military counter-revolution to drive out the invaders. In Egyptian history, this began a three-hundred-year period of renewed military influence and relative political independence, lasting until the conquest of Egypt by Alexander the Great around 332 B.C.

With respect to great karmic cycles, this was an important time for the development of consciousness in the cradle of Mediterranean/Mesopotamian culture, and for the beginning of a new karmic thrust of Egyptian influence. The general flow of at least one branch of this collective karma moved forward from Egypt through Rome to England. Another notable subcollective karmic complex radiated out from an historic battle fought on the Plain of Megiddo in southern Judea, also called the "Plain of Armageddon."

The story *Armageddon* was recorded in Western history as the result of a dramatic reference in the Bible, in the *Book of Kings*. This reference tells of the total destruction of King Josiah and his army of Judea on the plain of Armageddon by an Egyptian army that was on its way to do battle with Babylon, having crossed the southern territory of Judea. Believing himself to be God-inspired, King Josiah led his army of 20,000 in a surprise night-attack against 200,000 seasoned Egyptian soldiers. The commanders of the Egyptian army were surprised by this attack, believing King Josiah and his army to be vassal subjects of the Egyptian pharaoh. This story lends credence to the idea that the archetype of *Armageddon* refers to self-destruction caused by a misguided religious self-righteousness. In fact, King Josiah possessed a certain madness.

Archeological history confirms that Necho II sent ships to navigate around Africa. He was also instrumental in a public works project to open the first Suez canal. We will cover the ongoing incarnations of Pharaoh Necho II later, in a study on American presidents. What is important to this study is that both *Psalmtic* and his son Necho II reincarnated in Rome around the time of Christ—both being mentioned in the Bible (as karmic magnetism would have it)—as *Caesar Augustus*, and his successor and son-in-law, *Tiberius*. The karma of an independent Judea was at hand; the karma of a dominant high culture in Rome continued.

Octavian, Caesar Augustus
(Sept. 23, 63 B.C.—Aug. 19, A.D. 14)

A careful study of the life and times of *Octavian/Caesar Augustus* reveals similarities in the general character and karma between this Roman political leader and pharaoh *Psalmtic*. Additional outside study may be necessary because *Caesar Augustus* had a complex life. This lifetime occurred at a great apogee, or power point, marking the downward flow of incarnating consciousness that preceded the time of the Christ advent. A karmically selected group gathered in Rome during this critical era, together expressing a collective consciousness of dominance on the material plane. Many souls with strong military karma incarnated around this transformational window of time in world history—including the former Alexander the Great, who lived again as Julius Caesar, and Philip II of Macedonia who lived again as Pompey.

Octavian was the adopted son of Julius Caesar. After his adoptive father's death, he negotiated his way, through popular military uprising and political maneuvering, to the top of the Roman king-of-the-mountain domination game. *Ocatvian's* leadership style included a religious and cultural element that resembled the leadership style of the Egyptian pharaoh *Psalmtic*. In 12 B.C. *Octavian* had himself appointed head of the Roman state religion as high priest (Pontifix Maximus). In 2 B.C., he received from the Roman Senate the title "Father of His Country."

The personal power we see in the karmic magnetism of *Caesar Augustus* as Roman conqueror is a vicarious extension of Roman karmic cultural influence, expressed through the consciousness and character of this strong soul's life. We sense the iron will-to-power that permeated the collective karmic consciousness of Rome at that time. This soldier and politician was in his element.

Octavian had a special interest in Egypt. After his army conquered Egypt, *Octavian* placed the administration of this new territory under his own personal authority. Over the years, he continued to relate to Egypt more as he would to an extended family than as he would to a mere province of Rome, thus revealing the karmic magnetism of a former Egyptian pharaoh.

The next two famous lives of this military and political genius could be described as softer and more mellow in character. What we are sensing is an upgrading vibration in the collective social evolution. This soul's next famous incarnation was in England in the seventeenth century, as the English republican military genius *Oliver Cromwell*. Although similar in its overall pattern, the spirit of this lifetime seems to have been lighter than what came before. Of course, the victims of revolution and civil war at that time might not agree with this interpretation.

84

Oliver Cromwell
(Apr. 25, 1599— Sept. 3, 1658)

Oliver Cromwell, one of the more important leaders in British history, was born in England in a time of tremendous political, economic and cultural change. The British karmic collective at that time carried a strong reincarnational influence from both revolutionary Egypt and Rome. This was the consequence of the struggle between aristocracy and religious factions, that moved toward—or, as in the case of Rome, away from—the development of a republican form of government. It was into this tangled political web that *Oliver Cromwell* incarnated.

One generation earlier, Queen Elizabeth I (whose study follows) had completed a thirty-year period of intense cultural growth that involved considerable political and religious strife. In an attempt to quell civil war, Queen Elizabeth passed a number of laws banning Catholics and suppressing separatist sects such as the Congregationalists (including the Puritans), of which *Cromwell* became a member. This was a time when many members of such religious groups left for the British colonies in America.

The talented young *Cromwell* became a soldier and politician in support of the Protestant cause. His election to Parliament at the age of thirty brought him into direct conflict with the oppressive laws of the Church of England and with the organized factions of the Presbyterian Church that were competing for a strong influence in Parliament. Through a series of clever military and political maneuvers, *Cromwell* eventually became the head of the new British republic as Lord Protector. He was a leading influence in the Long Parliament at the time of the civil war that led to the execution of King Charles I.

As head of the government under a new constitution, *Cromwell* was instrumental in rewriting and reforming the laws of England. As part of this process, he helped create a broader basis for the Church that allowed members of various sects to worship outside the official Church. These efforts contributed to the strengthening of British prestige and to state tolerance in religious matters—which even extended to the Jews, who had not been allowed to settle in England since 1290.[10] *Cromwell*, who had deep religious commitments, grew more tolerant in his later years. Although a Puritan, he did not use state law to ban music, wine or dancing either at court or throughout the land. By the end of his life, strong character traits emerged reflecting the development

---

[10] Remember that the former Pharaoh Psalmtic was at the "karmic root" of a 700 B.C. Egyptian/Judean treaty.

of a higher form of statesman, as opposed to a lower form of military or political opportunist.

After *Cromwell's* death, the British civil war continued. When the monarchy was restored to power, Charles II (son of the executed Charles I) had *Cromwell's* body disinterred, hanged and beheaded. The karmic as well as metaphysical meaning of such an official demonstration cannot to be underestimated. One interpretation is that this soul can be "excused from class," allowing him the karmic choice—and, in a sense, freedom—to separate from the collective karma of England. This is a concept that you may wish to take into meditation.[11]

In this soul's next life in Egypt, we see what appears to be a life expended in the payment of even older karmic debt.

Mohammed Anwar el Sadat
(Dec. 25, 1918—Oct. 6, 1981)

A graduate of the Royal Military Academy of Cairo (a British-protectorate institution at the time), *Anwar el Sadat* became active in the Egyptian independence movement. He worked suc-

---

[11] Topics for meditation could be: What does intuition reveal concerning social sanction—including mockery, excommunication, or even execution? What are the considerations here? Would this be an analysis of the karmic potency of the collective will or of the individual will? Does collective karma overwhelm individual choice? Is spiritual maturity a factor?

cessfully with a group of Egyptian army officers against British occupation and was elected president of Egypt in 1970. Many have commented that *Sadat* was one of the more noble senior statesmen of our time. His assassination by Moslem extremists can be viewed as a tragedy for Egypt and for the peace process in the Middle East.

Sadat's life is a mirror of karmic loops stretching across the ages. In a karmic sense, this soul is now free or, may choose to be free, of an ancient Egyptian karma. It appears that he chose to "walk the karmic walk"—to repay the karmic debt—one life at a time.

Although not a spiritual initiate in the higher, classical sense, *Sadat* can be considered a strong soul as the result of the karmic leadership dharma that he pursued over many lifetimes. We see this soul as having the potential to become a great leader in some distant earth history, as of yet unplayed. Keep in mind that, compared with the muddle that our karmic personas tend to make here on earth, the spiritual soul is above it all in the eyes of divinity.

As you meditate on this soul progression, a hint concerning the complex political karma of *Anwar el Sadat* may be found by recalling that it was *Psalmtic*, father of Necho II, who arranged the original protectorate relationship between Egypt and Judea, about 700 B.C., against the common enemy of Babylon. The twentieth century reflects the karmic progression of a particular Egyptian/Judean, Mesopotamian/Babylonian and Greco-Roman cycle of social conflict and warfare. We will cover the biblical story (Se*cond Book of Kings*) of King Josiah of Judea and the archetypal story of *Armageddon* in a later study. However, a partial replay of that karmic era occurred when certain leaders from Judean history reincarnated in Germany to participate in a conflict repetition that resulted in World War II. This illustrates the karmic principle, "those who live by the sword die by the sword" or "a kingdom built with a sword will fall by the sword." As we stay with this subject, it becomes easier to see.

Elizabeth and Charles
The End of an Era

When we meditate on the lives and karma of individuals who represent nations—such as monarchs or other royalty—we are reflecting on a collective karma. For example, the conditions affecting the British monarchy at the end of the twentieth century are a direct reflection of British collective karma. However, whatever the collective wishes the individual soul must also accept.[12] Thus, the magnetic draw of a karmic collective that nurtures, for example, a strongly favorable attitude toward monarchy can attract former charismatic—or problematic—leaders into its royal family. This assumes the karmic cooperation, in some higher way, of the soul who is so called.

An example of this phenomena is the case of *Queen Elizabeth II* of England, who is responsible for some unfinished national business—including the Irish question. In addition, a renewed opportunity (in terms of reincarnation) for personal karmic choice is now available to *Elizabeth's* son *Prince Charles*. The karmic connection between the two of them has to do with their histories as queen and king, respectively. Not to burden this study with excess commentary, nor to defend it unnecessarily, we will simply present it and allow it to define itself. Those unfamiliar with the historical lives of *Elizabeth I* and *Charles I,* of England are advised to review their biographies.

The reign of *Queen Elizabeth I* marked the beginning of the modern British Commonwealth. Her era also saw the beginning of the British Protestant invasion of North Ireland. The present era reflects the ending of the cycle of these past karmic impulses. Ireland will again become whole and independent and the British Commonwealth, in a "royal crown" sense, will cease to exist as a unified whole. (This is meant as a prophetic probability.)

The soul of *Elizabeth I* was called into the stream of British collective karma to reincarnate at the height of the British empire, in

---

[12] All individuals and collectives are also, and always, part of greater collectives of individuals and groups.

the monarchical line. *Elizabeth I* was a strong, fearless, independent woman who took her responsibilities seriously. She would allow nothing to weaken her authority—including a state marriage.

Elizabeth I, Queen of England
(Sept. 7, 1533—Mar. 24, 1603)

Elizabeth II, Queen of England
(Apr. 21, 1926—)

Queen Elizabeth II, although from a different gene pool and with different childhood developmental influences, is the incarnation of her namesake *Elizabeth I*. She has many of the same characteristics: responsible, independent-minded, authoritarian, regal, manipulative.

What psychic potency, what power of myth, expresses through the British crown? According to British mythology, the crown of British monarchs is known as the "crown of David"—referring, of course, to the crown of biblical King David. The royal myth is that Jesus was a claimant to the crown of David, and possibly even a reincarnation of King David. In addition, Joseph of Arimethea, (perhaps the uncle of Jesus) brought the cup from the Last Supper as well as the mystic Holy Grail to England. According to royal myth, British monarchy is the legitimate defender of the Holy Grail and of the Christian faith. The longevity and prosperity of the British crown is due, in part, to the clarity and purity of this particular vision of the past.[13] However, the root of the

---

[13] Every Christian monarchy has held a similar self-validating myth. Never mind that Jesus stated in biblical texts that the prince of this world shall have no part in the kingdom of God. Could this mean that the position of prince, as a job description, is not valid in the "kingdom to come on earth"? If so, all types of Christian monarchies would be karmic relics, soon to end.

karma and myth of the British throne actually goes back to Egyptian aristocracy.

The grand galactic cycle of the turning of the ages has allowed a time of completion for remnant energies of old forms of consciousness. Over the last two thousand years, old leadership styles, such as the military feudal order, have continued to transform, upgrade, purify—whatever was necessary to stay in the game. Princedom after princedom was established, always by the sword, only to be swept away in time. Throughout history, willful and karmically misguided souls promoted old forms of dominating government, only to watch them later disappear. These efforts are still continued by a few.

Elizabeth II sits at the end of an era. The British empire is all but gone. Two elements of unfinished business concerning the British monarchy are still carried by this royal family. One is the Irish question; the other pertains to a past social-moral karmic problem that we will examine in the following section.

90

Charles I, King of England
(1600—1649)

Charles, Prince of Wales
(Nov. 14, 1948—)

Prince Charles is a reincarnation of *King Charles I*, England's executed king. Although *Charles* is a very public person, he nevertheless retains a shy, retiring side, neither inviting nor necessarily deserving public scrutiny. The following presentation is not intended as an invasion of personal space. The choices that are spread before this personality can be better understood by reviewing the biography of *Charles I.*

This life, for both *Charles* and *Elizabeth,* appears to be one of grace and not of negative karma. Is the British collective resisting the future? The answer is probably not any more than did other past-era Christian collectives of continental Europe or Russia. Change is at hand. It is logical that the great queen who presided over the beginning of the English Commonwealth would be honored in its last chapter as well.

These are the dramas a unified collective performs for itself while it is still harnessed by a wave of past karmic expectation. The British are slow to change, as were their past-life Greco-Roman and Egyptian predecessors. In fact, this aristocracy is the most iconoclastic "royal karmic remnant" in the world.

In the media, we have enjoyed humorous comments about the British monarchy as an on-going soap opera. In their next lives, these souls are likely to pursue their private lives beyond the burdens of public obligation. It is equally likely that the charismatic energy of their past lives will continue to lend an aura of presence to their persons. Public charisma is often no more than a magnetism charged by unconscious collective recognition.

Sholem Asch
Media in the Twentieth Century

During the twentieth century, we have witnessed the birth and coming of age of the mass media. The United States, and particularly California, has led the world in what can only be called a *karmic charge* into new territories, in terms of social influence in the media. American cultural influence—for better or for worse—has spread into every corner of the world psyche. Many highly karmic souls have chosen, by karmic debt, or by some sense of duty, to be involved in this unprecedented spread of culture and influence. Some very talented and artistic souls are on hand although, on the whole, the impact of public media on collective consciousness has had a rough start.

No other time, culture or people has dealt with such overwhelming impressions as are broadcast in the media today. Books, magazines, motion pictures and television carry tremendous potential to manipulate individual choices and, thus, the direction of cultural forms. The future karma of humankind will be greatly influenced by this new social platform—whether it be for great public good or great public harm. In and of itself, new technology holds an equal potential for public good and public evil. In a hundred years we will have a better understanding of its collective impact.

The long-range karmic consequences for individuals who perform in the public media today may be greater than during any other historical era. Because thought forms and emotions cling to the person who has expressed them, karma is affected by a movie performance in a way that is similar to having actually lived such a life. Psychologists have remarked that the unconscious does not recognize a joke. Similarly, it does not recognize the difference between acting and real life. We must ask what the impact on one's karma would be if one played an evil character in a movie—or a redeeming character, for that matter.

One who has participated in an adverse psychodrama in the past may choose to enter a field of public expression in the arts or media in a new life. In an attempt to redeem negative karma attached to a past persona, a creative soul may wish to attract public love or forgiveness. For example, in this age of mass media, the original *Judas* in the great passion play of Christ has reincarnated as an author and playwright in New York City.

Sholem Asch
(Nov. 1, 1880—July 10, 1957)

Born in Kutno, Poland, *Sholem Asch* immigrated to the United States at the turn of the twentieth century. Taking up his pen, he found great success in New York City as the first Yiddish playwright to achieve international fame. A supporter and publicist for Jewish and Zionist causes, he visited Israel and wrote about Zionist pioneers as early as 1907.

93

Many of Asch's Jewish fans were greatly distressed when he began writing a series of novels, called collectively his "Christological" series, during and after World War II: *The Nazarene* (1939), *The Apostle* (1943) and *Mary* (1949) and *Moses* (1951). Even though these novels are among his best literary works, many of *Asch's* former associates and supporters believed he was undergoing a breakdown. After he wrote his moving and popularly acclaimed novel (perhaps a "call" to understanding and forgiveness) he was abandoned by most of his New York Jewish supporters. Students of this case are encouraged to read *The Nazarene* for a better understanding of this karmic progression.

Eventually, *Asch* made amends to the Jewish community by writing plays and novels rooted in non-Christological themes. A naturalized U.S. citizen, *Asch* moved to Israel in 1955 to complete his life. He passed over in 1957.

This soul, who was the original *Judas*, lived an earlier life in Europe as *Uriel da Costa*.

Uriel da Costa
(1590—1647)

Judas
Disciple of Jesus

Uriel da Costa (or *Acosta*) was born in Oporto, Portugal in the late sixteenth century. His original name was *Gabriel da Costa*. He was born to a family that had been forcibly converted from Judaism to Catholicism. Very bright, and with a talent for writing, his life story is somewhat tragic.

94

The Acosta family moved to Holland at his urging so that they could convert back to Judaism. Following an independent path intellectually, *Acosta* came into conflict with the Amsterdam Jewish community and was excommunicated. He later recanted and was re-accepted. Then he restated his independent position again, and again was excommunicated, enduring great personal humiliation. He eventually took his own life.

This life study reveals an important connection. *Uriel da Costa* was an influence on the religious philosopher Benedict de Spinoza, who later was also excommunicated by the Amsterdam Synagogue. (Spinoza's study follows.) What is important about this connection is that Spinoza's spiritual origins were (like those of John the Baptist and William Blake) from the angel line of evolution. The name *Uriel* is the name of an archangel. *Acosta's* birth name, *Gabriel*, is also the name of an archangel.

Like that of *Judas*, the life of *Uriel Acosta* was tragic. He faced issues about the freedom of religious belief and loyalty, the same issues that tragically overshadowed the life of the disciple *Judas* whose karma was to play the role of Jesus Christ's betrayer. *Judas* loved and followed John the Baptist, as did many of the early followers of Jesus. John the Baptist, we recall, completed his last life as Kahlil Gibran, at an almost simultaneous location and time as did *Sholem Asch*, in early twentieth century New York City.

Jane Seymour
A Past Life Legacy

The United States, especially from the 1950s onward, has led in an explosion of the creative use of electronic technologies, enhancing all forms of public communication. World centers of creative influence, aided by public media, exist in New York City, Los Angeles and Chicago—centers driven by money, power and social influence. Southern California, in particular, has emerged as an area with great influence over the evolution of human consciousness. This area will remain a cradle of the New Age throughout most of the next century.

Because it has been located at a spiritual and psychic crossroads for the past fifty years, Hollywood has drawn talented people from around the world. It has become a mixing bowl of cultures, as charismatic souls who incarnated in California and elsewhere have migrated to this magnetic center of creative public expression. The desire for fame, to be on the leading edge of a change-wave in the consciousness of humanity and to live in a land where creativity abounds has attracted many. The openness of California culture, with its relatively lax social expectations, has allowed for an atmosphere of experimentation and opportunity. Nevertheless, where there is much creativity, there is also much struggle.

In reviewing the Akashic Records, we find examples of formerly famous persons being drawn, in this life, into public entertainment careers. The focus of this and the next several studies is to emphasize the role of karmic fame as both an enhancer of personal talent and a contributor to natural charisma. In the Hollywood of the 1940s and 1950s, for example, it was not so difficult for an unknown young actor or actress to enter the society of the famous, find an opportunity to be tested and, with a little luck, be discovered. The next several studies demonstrate this phenomenon. We begin with an example of a serendipitous discovery.

A young British actress, *Jane Seymour*, had just changed her name. This would be her stage name; she felt strangely drawn to it. As it turned out, this name change focused a spotlight on her career. At a party, she was introduced to a filmmaker as the actress *Jane Seymour.* He was very responsive. "Don't I know you?" he asked. "Haven't I seen you in such-and-such a part?" The young actress seemed familiar to him. That party introduction resulted in a test for a part that became *Jane Seymour's* first major role. Was it magic?

Actress Jane Seymour   Jane Seymour, Queen of England
(Feb. 15, 1951—)   (1509—Oct. 24, 1537)

We find that this well-known and internationally loved film and television actress is a reincarnation of her famous namesake, the sixteenth century British queen, *Jane Seymour.* How is that for karmic magnetism? Although this person unconsciously called on a past-life energy to enhance her present career, there is little or no karmic connection between these two life situations. *Jane Seymour's* present close family members are not incarnated from British monarchy.[14]

An aura of natural goodness surrounds *Jane Seymour* in her present life. Her past-life persona, the queen, was honored by burial in Westminster Cathedral next to her husband King Henry

---

[14] It is interesting that this actress's present television role, set in the American wild West, is entitled *Dr. Quinn, Medicine Woman.* As a phonetic correspondence, Dr. *Quinn* played by Jane Seymour would become with a play on words, "Dr. *Queen"* Seymour—Medicine Woman.

the VIII, who was the controversial founder of the British Protestant reformation. *Queen Jane* was honored as a leader in the psychodrama surrounding the founding of the British Anglican Church. The magnetism of the prayers and compassion expressed by millions is an undeniable influence in her present life.

Both *Jane Seymours* have used fame and fortune to contribute to the greater collective evolution and well-being through various charitable acts. The actress *Jane Seymour* has chosen her parts with an eye to social contribution. Is it possible that she intuits her connection to the British queen? Such is often the case among formerly famous individuals.

Elizabeth Taylor
Forever Cleopatra

Our next study looks at the life of a famous Egyptian queen who was reborn in England in the early 1930s. This beautiful, talented charismatic child actress was drawn to the film industry in Hollywood. During the course of a phenomenal acting career, she was offered an opportunity to play Cleopatra, a major movie role—and a dramatized version of her own past life. We refer, of course, to *Elizabeth Taylor*, international film star and present day queen of Hollywood. This is not a new or unusual revelation. Many seers, psychics and mystics over the years have commented that *Elizabeth Taylor* really was *Cleopatra VII,* queen of Egypt, in a former life.[15]

99

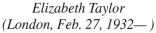
Elizabeth Taylor
(London, Feb. 27, 1932—)

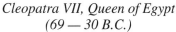
Cleopatra VII, Queen of Egypt
(69 — 30 B.C.)

At the time of *Cleopatra VII* of Egypt, we also find the Roman military commander, Pompey, who reincarnated in the United States in the mid twentieth century, and Julius Caesar, who was reborn at the end of the nineteenth century in the state of Arkan-

---

[15] Others have also claimed to be, or have been told by psychics that they were, reincarnations of the famous queen. It is always possible that such persons may be modeling the karmic complex; but there was only one original.

sas. This former Japanese shogun became General Douglas MacArthur, one of the most dramatic and successful military commanders in U.S. history.

Elizabeth Taylor has had little interaction with her former lovers from the Roman era. All, however, have shared an awareness of one another in their present lives through the medium of fame. Part of the mystery of the life of *Cleopatra VII* in 50 B.C. is that she was a reincarnation of another *Cleopatra* who lived in Greece around 350 B.C. This other *Cleopatra* was the young wife of the aging father of Alexander the Great, Philip II of Macedonia, an earlier incarnation of Pompey. Alexander the Great reincarnated as Julius Caesar. When the entire karmic script comes into view, all the parts make more sense.

Haydn and Neil Diamond
Classic and Pop

This study will require intuitive receptivity on the part of many. We will meditate on the effect of time, culture and attitude on the destiny and character of incarnating talent. In eighteenth and nineteenth century Europe, musical careers were developed from an early age with intense discipline. The teachers of that era were often harsh and even sometimes abusive toward their students, as the following case illustrates.

Franz Josef Haydn
(Mar. 31, 1732—May 31, 1809)

Neil Diamond
(Jan. 24, 1941—)

Josef Haydn was one of the greatest composers of the classical period of European music. For young *Haydn*, music and survival were linked. His early childhood was characterized by difficulty and even desperation, often involving actual hunger. By our present-day standards, the world of his childhood seems cruel.

One's parent, family, culture, astrological influences and other unseen karmic choices all contribute to major differences in personality expression and ambition. In contrast with the eighteenth century world of *Haydn* the unguided development of musical talent in the United States around 1950 to 1970 allowed for a much less burdened persona. The modern-day culture of plenty and play provided fundamentally different building blocks for a musical career. Talent, even latent genius, was allowed to emerge at a more natural rate of development.

The American pop artist, songwriter-singer *Neil Diamond*, began his career by writing made-to-order songs for other performers. This past-life connection provides an interesting and insightful meditation opportunity for the discerning student of reincarnation. *Neil Diamond,* the former *Josef Haydn*, has a strong influence on the Hollywood music elite and continues to play pop music, both vocal and instrumental, at sold-out concerts around the world.

John Lennon
Charisma of a Genius

This past-life study is historically complex and touches on serious cultural prejudice. The public history of this star-crossed soul spans six famous lives over two millennia, weaving a strange and fascinating blend of social popularity, genius, madness and personal disaster. Some of its mystery comes from a life rooted in biblical mythology. Once a life has been linked to, or captured in, sacred literature, that soul is often called back to the social arena by a subtle and irresistible karmic magnetism, whether it is ready or not. In this way, a past-life connection to sacred literature can amplify karma.

The first historically accessible life that was recorded in public literature and that is relevant for this study can be found in the Bible in I and II *Maccabees*. Your study of this case should begin with a rereading of the charismatic, revolutionary Jewish passion-play of the *Maccabee* revolt against the Greco-Persian empire of Antiocus IV.

| *Jonathan the Maccabee* | *Niccolo Machiavelli* |
| *(c. 160 B.C.)* | *(May 3, 1469—June 22, 1527)* |

We find in *Jonathan the Maccabee* a political astuteness that, as leader of the *Maccabee* cause after the death of his older brother, allowed him to negotiate a critical political settlement. Playing

Greece, Rome and the Persian empire against one another, he established a degree of independence for Judea. This Old Testament story is a karmic model for the pre-Christian revolutionary ideal. Its political motif has continued to influence countless generations of Bible readers.

The soul of *Jonathan the Maccabee* re-emerged on the historical stage in the fifteenth century as the famous *Niccolo Machiavelli*. This Italian Renaissance writer and statesman expressed a persistent gift, perhaps even genius, for public service and political activism, as well as strong personal ambition.

The magic of *Niccolo Machiavelli's* career, and his rise to the top as a loved and competent political advisor, was due in part to the magnetic charisma of a karmic rootedness in biblical history. His writings are a creative exposition on the use and abuse of power.

One is advised to study *Machiavelli's* life and meditate on this amazing confluence of karma, both public and personal, until it has been fully grasped. What karmic energy did he call forth to follow him into other lives by writing his famous booklet *Il Principe*? It was probably written to impress Caesar Borgia, from whom *Machiavelli* was seeking an advisory position, but did his advice to the political dictator have a positive or deleterious karmic effect? *Machiavelli* wrote on the opposite side as well; in other writings, he advocated a citizen army. He even became actively involved in recruiting and directing such a force during that lifetime.

104

This soul next appeared in England as the famous populist politician *John Wilkes*. In our study of this case, we can sense the diplomatic skill, genius, passion, ambition, frustration, disappointment and potentially crushing karmic weight of this next life.

The complex and complementary record of the lives of *John Wilkes* and *Niccolo Machiavelli* cannot be presented in a few words. As the researcher compares these two lives, a constant stream of instruction concerning karmic patterns is presented to the intuition.[16]

---

[16] Other former Maccabee brothers incarnated in France; brother Simon, for example, became the famous, or infamous, Cardinal Richelieu, advisor to the French king.

John Wilkes was one of the founders of British political radicalism. He served in Parliament on several occasions and was seen as a controversial thorn in the royal behind. He launched fearless, relentless attacks on the British king and his advisors in a periodical called the *North Briton*. Although he had more integrity than most of his contemporaries, he was accused of engaging in political and financial misdealings. He was hailed as a hero by the common folk, but later lost popularity when he directed the London police in suppressing a riot. This pragmatic tendency to switch sides may have had an impact on his next tragic life as American actor *John Wilkes Booth*.

A careful study of the life of *John Wilkes*, including his private escapades with the Monks of Medmenham Abbey, as well as of his preceding two lives (*Jonathan the Maccabee* and *Niccolo Machiavelli*), reveals the logic behind his next three tragic lives.

John Wilkes	*John Wilkes Booth*
(Oct. 17, 1727—Dec. 26, 1797)	*(May 10, 1838—Apr. 26, 1865)*

The British *John Wilkes* had a decadent, playboy side. He would go slumming with a small group of friends for long bouts of wine, women and song. A bitter root of alcoholism and self-abuse attached itself to him with a firm karmic hold. Perhaps as a result of such dissipation, this star of the public stage entered life again for a short time in the United States as the troubled, possibly emotionally disturbed, intensely ambitious, tragic stage actor *John*

Wilkes Booth. The phonetic and psychic correspondence between these two names is interesting.

The life of *John Wilkes Booth* can be evaluated as an intense encounter with a "karmic bullet." Frustrated ambition and talent, an indiscriminate and willful commitment to a political cause and a wild urge to follow his beliefs without regard for the consequences led to disaster. *John Wilkes Booth* is notorious as the assassin of President Abraham Lincoln, who was an incarnation of an arhat.

Born to a family of professional stage actors, the young *John W. Booth* was submerged in the dramatic emotion of Shakespearean tragedy that permeated the emotional platform of his life. Intellectual opportunism, without ethical discrimination, found *Booth* siding with the Southern cause. As a hidden personal agenda, he may also have been pursuing political opportunity in the newly created independent Southern Confederacy. Early during the civil war years, *Booth* secretly became an agent for the British, who were conspiring to divide the United States. By the end of the war, possible madness, coupled with alcoholic bingeing, led *Booth* to become involved in a dramatic, ill-conceived plan to kidnap the president of the United States.

This soul's karmic experience as an incidental assassin (the original plan had been to kidnap the president, not murder him) set an adverse karmic tone for his next two lifetimes. By developing as full an evaluation as possible of the life of *John Wilkes Booth* and his preceding lives, we can better establish an intuitional springboard leading to an understanding of his next life in Russia.

In this soul's next immediate incarnation, as a young boy in late nineteenth century Russia, he experienced the tragedy of seeing a loved older brother suffer government execution by public hanging. This brother, along with several other revolutionaries, had been caught in a conspiracy to assassinate the Czar.

The name of this boy who watched his brother hang was *Vladimir Ilyich Ulyanov*, the future Russian Bolshevik leader.

Later, with dramatic revolutionary flair, he adopted the pseudonym *Lenin*—meaning "iron."

Vladimir Ilyich Lenin
(April 22, 1870—Jan. 21, 1924)

John Winston Lennon
(Oct. 9, 1940—Dec. 8, 1980)

A biographical review of the life of *Lenin* is important. While living in Switzerland, the young *Lenin* published a revolutionary, anti-royalist, socialist magazine called *Iskra* (*The Spark*). Photos of *Lenin* in a wheelchair in the mid 1920s, after the Russian civil war and at the end of his life, seem to cry out: "what happened to the revolution?" Had he been no more than a circus "ring master," directing a performance that amounted to one of the greatest political frauds in world history?

In his next incarnation, karma sent him back into a turning-point life, once again in England. This time, he began a rock and roll band in the streets of London with some old pals from *John Wilkes'* time (the Merry Monks of Medmenham Abbey). The challenge of drug and alcohol addiction and excess continued as a theme of this life.

The dark side of life is shielded by a thick veil. When anyone crosses over to serve the dark forces, we see them drop into a murky pool. We can, however, identify these souls as they re-emerge into the light in another life. Such souls are given an opportunity by grace to reclaim their karmic life course. They have the choice to pay their debts and continue on with the greater community of souls who belong to the "light" side of life.

To have taught against—or assumed pseudo-authority to replace—God Spirit in the guidance of humanity represents a serious adverse karma. There is no punishment, exactly. The soul is left to go its own way, beset by old visions and met by old desires. Angels always help mitigate the fall, within the limits of the laws that rule grace. One must receive what is willed within the law.

You are advised to study the life of Beatle superstar *John Lennon*. This is an interesting case, in part, because of *Lennon's* participation in, and impact on, the Euro-American counter culture of the l960s and 1970s. In reviewing his life, we see a karmic tumble in the form of a personal disintegration on the public stage. Questions to consider include: What were the possible opportunities for his talents? What role did indiscriminate drug use have? What role did Yoko Ono play in *Lennon's* life?

We find that Yoko Ono was a "copy" of a *Lenin* nemesis, a Russian nihilist who was convicted of stalking and attempting to kill the young party leader. There is a karmic mystery here. Friends have said that *Lennon* was strangely mesmerized by Yoko. Love obsession is a potent emotion as well as a karmic magnet. In some ways, Yoko may have orchestrated the end of *Lennon's* family life—a possible source of grace for him. For example, *Lennon's* son Julian was a reincarnation of the loved older brother of *Vladimir Ulyanov* who was hung by the Czar.[17]

In 1980, *John Lennon* was gunned down by a former mental patient in New York City in front of the Dakota apartment building. A possible karmic significance to the name of this place of

---

[17] A clue to an even deeper mystery is found in a favorite chair collected by *John Lennon* and Yoko Ono. It is an exact replica of the Egyptian royal crown chair of Tutankhamon. This chair's design originated in the life of the Pharaoh Akhenaten, possibly Tutankhamon's older brother, who was the great Egyptian political/religious reforming pharaoh of l340 B.C. Mystically speaking, this is the archetypal chair of King David; Akhenaten's life reflects the real archetypal and karmic passion play story of the mythical "King David" of the Bible.

death was that *Lennon* loved the state of South Dakota, and actually wished to live there. Mount Rushmore National Park, where the giant stone sculpture of four American presidents is located, is in South Dakota. President Abraham Lincoln's image is carved into the stone of the Mount Rushmore Memorial. Thus, the circle closes with a striking example of a *karmic signature.*

This former errant actor, who took the life of President Lincoln, had his life taken in a similar manner two incarnations later. Having paid the debt indicates spiritual release and is a sign that he is still sheltered by grace; not paying the debt could indicate that evil prevails. We remember that there is no absolute punishment—only grace. Likewise, there is no absolute death—only growth. Life does not produce innocence; it does produce experience. And angels work overtime.

Akhenaten's life story was mantled by an arhat energy predicating a coming change of the great galactic age, 1340 years before the main event, the great passion play of Christ. The entrenched Egyptian priesthood of Amun resisted Pharoah Akenaten and his leadership. They coveted and conspired against his throne—symbolized by his chair. Many of the priests who originally resisted, and eventually overthrew, Pharoah Akhenaten's reforms, have been caught up in a three-millennial-long karmic wave of spiritual resistance.

The potent karmic magnetism that accompanied the end of this great age cycle has brought many of these same souls to be tempted, again and again, to become unwitting leaders in causes that continue to resist the advancing solar light and the universal leadership of Christ. Being caught in a wave of resistance to spiritual reforming energy is like being caught in a psychic rip tide that can carry the swimmer away from shore and out to sea. We will cover the story of Pharaoh Akhenaten and the crisis of 1340 B.C. in a later study.

Bruce Willis

Acting in History

The father of John Wilkes Booth, *Junius Brutus Booth* was a British actor who brought his rendition of the Shakespearean play *Richard III* to the United States in the 1840s. His sons all became actors, specializing in tragic drama.

The soul of *Junius Booth* lived, in an earlier life, as a minor, historically anonymous and rebellious character in the original Maccabee drama. He also had a life as a similar character in the fifteenth century British popular uprising against King Richard III.[18] He had an additional life, again in England, as a part-time stage actor and social outsider during the era of the regicides—a name for those who participated in the rebellion against aristocracy and demanded the execution of Charles I.

In the late seventeenth century, this soul incarnated in England again, this time as a more accomplished actor of Shakespearean drama. The part of Brutus in Shakespeare's *Julius Caesar* was one "linkage" to the name Brutus.[19]

Junius Brutus Booth has reincarnated in the present time. This soul has become the internationally recognized star of stage and screen, *Bruce Willis*.

One of *Bruce Willis'* many major movie roles was in the international hit *Die Hard*, in which a group of thieves pretended to be terrorist revolutionaries. This life leads us back to the preceding sequence of lives; in particular, that of Vladimir Ilich Ulyanov and the Bolshevik revolution. The Bolshevik cause, sponsored

---

[18] In the Maccabee drama, the original father of the clan was Mattathias of Modin. Although not a part of this immediate study, we find this same one—Mattathias—incarnated in the real-life Richard III drama as the rebel leader Wat Tyler; look it up.

[19] He did not have a life as a Roman during the actual time of Julius Caesar.

and secretly financed by cynical, opportunistic Western capitalists, was from its very inception more of a robbery than a revolution. Did Lenin know? Did he conspire? Or was he a true believer, an opportunist using foreign money for a better end? It is not known if Lenin consciously concealed one of the greatest transfers of wealth in world history.

Junius Brutus Booth
(May 1, 1796—Nov. 30, 1852)

Bruce Willis
(March 19, 1955—)

Die Hard presents an evil—but clever—antagonist, against whom *Bruce Willis'* character (cowboy) must struggle in a desperate battle. Without the conscious intention of the movie's producers, or of *Bruce Willis*, the arch villain, the leader of the terrorists, took on elements of the historical John Wilkes Booth. Observe the anti-hero's caped fall from the building as it merges, in psychic image, with *Booth's* dramatic jump onto the stage of the Ford Theater after the shooting of Lincoln. The merged characters, from the movie and from history, dissolve psychically into a sea of collective memory. Thus, the movie presents an unconscious element: an unrevealed version of Vladimir Ilich Ulyanov's lead in a well-planned, well-financed raid on the Romanov treasury.

The *Bruce Willis* movie *Die Hard* may be an unconscious revelation about the hidden secret of the Bolshevik revolution; however, one must see the movie to appreciate this observation. There are no real secrets in the long run. Love must bare the truth in preparing the way to forgiveness. Collective memory pushes for openings through the veil of public darkness and denial—even in the movies.

Stephen King
Writers in the Popular Media

In the next two case studies, we identify three lives each for two well-known Greek classical playwrights from antiquity, *Aristophanes* and *Aeschylus*. As modern contemporaries, these two prolific writers have both had a strong influence on popular consciousness through the creative channel of Hollywood's film and television industries. We begin with *Aristophanes*.

Aristophanes, Greek Playwright
(450—388 B.C.)

One of the greatest genius wordsmiths in history, *Aristophanes* was an early Grecian craftsman and inventor in the field of public performance. He competed successfully for honors and prizes awarded to the winners of the public play contests of ancient Athens. Known for his humor, satire and sharp wit in support of conservative social values, *Aristophanes'* form of satire included clever attacks and parodies that targeted famous persons.

Aristophanes' use of the written word placed him among the major contributors to the early art forms, both written and spoken. It is said that imitators of *Aristophanes* in the early Roman period spread his influence throughout Western culture. *Aristophanes* emphasized the absurdity of human pretension, as well as the absurdity of placing other people or one's culture on a pedestal. As a social humorist, he can be called an "equal-opportunity leveler" for taking shots at both reputable and disreputable persons alike. For example, one of his plays mocked—and, thereby, discredited—Socrates, one of the great Athenian moral philosophers.

We find a Grecian karmic influence in Dublin, Ireland. An even stronger karmic influence, which included a dominate Roman-karmic energy not present in the Dublin psychic milieu, was present in early eighteenth century London. With the mixed soul energy of both Athens and Rome, London at that time was a magnet for literary renaissance.[20] The early to mid-eighteenth century was also when the American Colonies rebelled against British domination. Socrates reincarnated in the colony of Pennsylvania, to become the well-known American inventor, statesman and genius Benjamin Franklin.

On a diplomatic mission to London, Franklin, an advocate of American independence, was arrested by the British authorities and put on trial. He only escaped with his freedom—and perhaps his life—due to an outcry by the British public, who loved him and demanded his release. Franklin returned to America to inform the Colonies that the British government could not be reasoned with. The American Declaration of Independence followed—a potential death sentence act. Franklin's trial for treason in London was a drama that duplicated, in many ways, the trial and condemnation of Socrates by the elders of Athens—a trial that ended in Socrates' condemnation and forced suicide. (More on Socrates follows in a later study.)

Aristophanes reincarnated in the seventeenth century as the British literary genius and satirist *Jonathan Swift*. *Aristophanes* and Socrates reincarnated in a similar era to deal with old Athenian karma.

Among the literary associates of *Jonathan Swift* were Sir Richard Steele, publisher of a popular London social tabloid *The Tatler*, and the poet Alexander Pope.[21] Pope, as you recall, was

---

[20] A study of the early eighteenth century English capital reveals an explosion of literary creativity and opportunity. Relaxed publishing laws contributed to this.

[21] As a side comment, Sir Richard Steele and his literary partner Joseph Addison were good friends and same-gender soulmates. This couple has since completed a life together in New York and California.

the former Greek poet Pindar. In his next life, Pope slipped into the world of dark and frightening imagery as the nineteenth century American poet Edgar Allen Poe. *Swift's* progress was similar to that of Poe.

Satire, the barbed targeting of others with social commentary, can be used to release tension and to point out the absurdity of pretension. Its humor can promote healing, but not if carried too far. If this type of wit becomes a primary part of one's consciousness, such dark humor can become a root of psychic cancer and a precursor of mental disease. Such a condition finally caught up with *Jonathan Swift*.

A master of understated irony and social satire, *Swift* ended his days in a mental institution. Was *Swift's* dementia merely the beginning of senility, a physical side effect of aging? In his case, it was more than that. Did those two things—his work and his mental condition—belong in the same category? In this case, spiritually speaking, they did. The life of *Jonathan Swift* was one of literary success and public acclaim that is still appreciated by many today, even though it ended on a spin into insanity. You are directed to study *Swift's* biography.

Jonathan Swift
(Nov. 30, 1667—Oct. 19, 1745)

Stephen Edwin King
(Sept. 21, 1949—)

We find this soul reincarnated in the United States today as the world-famous novelist *Stephen King* who is an internationally acclaimed writer of horror novels. A major influence in Hollywood, he has affected the dreams and imaginations of countless millions of readers as well as movie and television viewers worldwide. Some of his credits include *Carrie* (1974; film, 1976), *The Shining* (1977; film, 1980) and *Misery* (1987; film, 1990).

Is there any indication that *Stephen King* recognizes, in a deep spiritual sense, what he has created and, thus, what he may be responsible for? Could his present life be a continuation of the conditions of a former institutionalized self? If so, how many lives could this continue through? Where could a fascination with the dark side lead him? Having asked these questions, we release them to the ethers in a way that does not require us to deal with the answers—or with more questions—or to follow them into the shadows of dark, unstable mental energies. May light illumine the way.

116

Aeschylus and Cervantes
Popular Playwright

Aeschylus, Greek dramatist
(c. 525 B.C.—456 B.C.)

Aeschylus, the author of some of the earliest surviving Greek tragedies, lived in an age when Greece was under threat of domination by the Persian empire. He fought in the battles of Marathon
(490 B.C.) and Salamis (500 B.C.). *Aeschylus* was a man immersed in the struggles of his culture and time. With great beauty
and grandeur of language, his plays were offered as dramatized
expressions of moral conflict as well as lofty religious emotions.

117

With his and many others' influence, the Grecian stage arts
evolved into spectacular expressions of public entertainment. Due
perhaps to the conservative Athenian social requirements for public performances, the plays were designed as public education to
evoke thoughtful contemplation about moral conflict. Contests
were also held for this purpose, honoring the best playwrights
with public awards.

Much that has come down to our time concerning *Aeschylus*
has been processed through the understanding of later generations, who elevated him to god-like status. *Aeschylus* was
inspired, no question about it. But was he a spiritual initiate,

an older soul in the spiritual sense, as we would understand it today?

This talented personality was a spirit-inspired channel for educational energies.[22] With a talent for wordsmithing, he incarnated in an opportune time and place to uplift the consciousness of Athenian society. This time in Greece, especially in Athens, represented a cradle of consciousness in human social evolution. It was also the era of Pythagoras, who preceded Socrates and Plato.

We see that the inspiration of *Aeschylus* was aided by higher spiritual powers. *Aeschylus'* expression of genius was greater than his actual personal karmic evolution. Although his work was exceptionally brilliant, he nevertheless had many more lives to live. He even wrote his own obituary, which was carved on his memorial stone. He said of himself that he had fought at Marathon and Salamis, but he made no mention of being a writer or having written plays.

We must "step down the power" in our assumptions about this former Greek (and former Vedic) playwright. His next famous life was in Spain as *Miguel Cervantes*, renowned author of *Don Quixote de la Mancha*, considered a masterpiece of world literature.

118

Miguel de Cervantes Saavedra
(Sept. 29, 1547—Apr. 23, 1616)

Born to a poor family in the Spanish university town of Alcala de Henares, in the time of Spanish military expansionism, during

---

[22] In an earlier life, this soul had also been a writer, a channel really, for early Vedic writings.

the Inquisition, *Miguel Cervantes Saavedra* first became a soldier. After being exposed to fine poetry and exciting public plays during his travels, he found himself drawn to drama. He determined to pursue the stage arts as a side occupation.

In reading biographical material, you may get a sense that the genius and talent expressed by *Miguel Cervantes* came from a deep, inexplicable root. This soul entered life with these gifts. However, his personal and family life was difficult. Plagued by financial disasters, he had a tragic life in many ways. Bankrupted and imprisoned, his greatest wish was for commercial success—a karmic desire.

We observe, as we once again "step down the power" in the bridge to his next life, that this soul is not yet an initiate. More that anything else, this highly talented soul wants, and perhaps needs, personal recognition and success.

The former *Miguel Cervantes Saavedra de Alcala de Henares* reincarnated in the twentieth century United States as *Steven J. Cannell*, one of the most prolific television sit-com writers and publishers in the history of Hollywood.

119

Steven J. Cannell
(Feb. 5, 1941—)

One of the most successful screen writers in the world, *Steven J. Cannell* has, at last, achieved social and economic prosperity and security. At the top of his field, *Cannell* has had as many as three current award-winning television serial dramas running simultaneously on the international television networks. His is one of the better examples of a past-life talent, with a driving karmic desire for success, who has entered a present life with access to opportunity.

Is *Steven Cannell* an idealist or a religious moralist in his writing? Not noticeably. However, some of his character portrayals reflect the pathos of the unsung—and often unstrung—heroism, and even the impractical idealism, expressed in the saga of *Don Quixote*. As for any spiritual element in his work, although *Cannell* may be religious, his expression is aimed only at the popular market.

Personal success and financial security are primary motivations in this case. What evidence of this tendency existed in the life of *Miguel Cervantes*? With a careful review of the biographical material, and with meditation, these past-life connections can become clear.

Addison and Steele
Same-Gender Soulmates

Joseph Addison and *Sir Richard Steele* were early eighteenth century British literary personalities who were same-gender soulmates. The purpose of this revelation is to examine the type of relationship possible between two same-gender soulmates who are linked by common interests and goals. These two were the polarities of one soul and present an interesting study when the various interactions and partnership support energies are noted in their biographies.

Joseph Addison
(1672—1719)

Sir Richard Steele
(1672—1729)

121

Joseph Addison was a clergyman, essayist, poet and statesman. He received a generous pension from his last public position as British Secretary of State. This much loved literary talent and social commentator was quite conservative and of good Christian conscience.

Sir Richard Steele was a novelist and dramatist who published a periodical *The Tatler*, and later *The Spectator,* in which both he and *Addison* wrote hundreds of articles and essays of general public interest. Their objective was to contribute to the educational and moral climate of British society.

As former Roman aristocrats, these two suffered a fall into sexual abuse and corruption, including banquets, slaves, multiple partners and orgies during the time of Emperor Nero. They were together many times, she (the feminine polarity) having been male more often than not. In an earlier life, they had lived in Athens, both as males, during a time of social, moral and literary renaissance and both wrote public plays.

In several other lives, they soldiered together and were caught up karmically in the excesses of war-time emotions together. They experienced the filial love of comrades-in-arms, as well as the bestial, bloody side of war—feelings they later drowned in alcohol and personal excess.

These two had many good and normal lives, as well. They were priests and priestesses, artists and rulers, as well as wise advisors and literary personalities. In many lives, in many centuries and many parts of the world, they were lovers.

In their lifetime in England, *Addison* and *Steele,* expressed a karmic need and spiritual commitment to contribute to the moral side of society—a task they accomplished. While sexual confusion and abuse had been an issue for them before, it was not so during this life. The male polarity (*Addison*) and the female polarity (*Steele*) of this soul couple supported one another in a most discernible way.

He did his best to express his true inner strength and spirit and avoid forms of Roman corruption. *She* nurtured their relationship in a perceptively female way—partnering his energies while expressing her own skills and karmic directions. Of the two of them, *she* was more the socialite, while *he* received greater recognition as a literary genius and minor master of English literature. In their early years, *she* joined the army. A zealous advocate of public morality, *she* published a booklet of religious devotion. *He* wrote poetry and entered the public service.

Both reincarnated in the United States in the early 1910s, this time destined to be together. This time *she* was *she* and *he* was *he.*

He entered the world of literature and poetry in 1920s New York bohemian society. Born to a wealthy and aristocratic New York family, *he* quickly abandoned that influence. Following *his* muse, *he* reopened old karmic patterns. *He* also became homosexual at an early age. Focusing on the development of *his* writing talent and fighting a tendency toward alcohol abuse, *he* eventually became an accomplished editor at a New York publishing house.

Born into a solid, upstanding family in New England, *she* (this time in a female body) wanted, more than anything, to be a good daughter and to please the social expectations of her society mother and university professor father. *She* also had latent homosexual tendencies. At an early age, *she* unhappily married a timid, artistic man. This unhappy marriage lasted nine years.

Not until *she* met *him,* did her life seem to have purpose and direction. *She* met *him* in a Greenwich Village coffee shop; *she* was with a girl friend, *he* was alone. A conversation started between them and continued for twenty-four hours without let-up. Seemingly coming from totally different perspectives (*he* wasn't attracted to women; *she* wasn't attracted to men, although *she* liked men), they merged mentally. Both were aware of a pull with the strength of a giant cosmic magnet. The attraction never abated.

Eventually, these two were able to establish heterosexual harmony and personal stability together. They married, both still in their mid-thirties, to live a life of mutual emotional support. At retirement, they relocated in California. Both were talented writers, although unknown in this life. *She* left a novel, as of yet unpublished, on the subject of cosmic twins and reincarnation. Partially clairvoyant and very intuitive, *she* used her ability to "see" in a creative way, and to imagine other lives (many of them partially autobiographical in nature), to build the characterizations in *her* novel. It is easy to predict that this novel will eventually be discovered and become a classic contribution to New Age perspectives on reincarnation and the karmic path of soulmates.

Ramses II and Nefertere
Egypt, England and California

The next study is another example of historically famous soulmates.[23]

Ramses II, Pharaoh of Egypt   *Henry II, King of England*
(1292—1225 B.C.)   *(1133—1189 A.D.)*

A review of the karmic history of *Ramses II* of Egypt is complicated by a centuries-old assumption that Moses of the Bible

124

---

[23] As a good example of syncronicity, at the time of this writing, a television program guide was circulated in newspapers in Southern California. On the front page of this programming guide was a photograph of the actual mummy of the Egyptian *Pharaoh Ramses II* (from 1250 B.C.). Public Broadcasting Service (P.B.S.) television was going to show a special documentary that coming Sunday evening on the life and times of *Ramses II*. In the same television guide, for that same Sunday evening, was another listing for a program running nearly simultaneously on a different television network; the movie entitled *Lion in Winter*, starring Katherine Hepburn as Eleanor of Aquitane and Peter O'Toole as the English king, *Henry II*. Although the actors involved, Hepburn and O'Toole, were not these original characters in history, it is interesting, even amazing, to note that *Henry II* of England was indeed a reincarnation of *Ramses II* of Egypt. The historical French/English queen, *Eleanor of Aquitane*, was a reincarnation of *Nefertere*, the former wife of the great pharaoh of Egypt, *Ramses II*. The convergence of these

lived at the time of *Ramses II*. This has not been confirmed by modern archeology or by Akashic research.

This couple has lived together again in California in the twentieth century. It was not a public or collective life. The former *Ramses/Henry* was a civil engineer, a public safety officer, who worked for and retired from the California Department of Transportation and died in the early 1970s. With a strong personality, unburdened in this incarnation by historical karma, he made his mark in the world in the field of freeway construction management, with a few important technical innovations to his credit. He had a high intelligence, moral character and religious temperament developed without the influence of excessive power or responsibility. His personality was, in many ways, similar to the persona of King *Henry II*. Remember that relative freedom from historical karma in one life does not mean that such karma is finished. Remnant karma will eventually be called forth to solicit repetition in another life. One's moral growth is the only defense.

125

Queen Nefertere of Egypt
Sister/Chief Wife of Ramses II
(c. 1250 B.C.)

Eleanor of Aquitane
Queen of England
(1122—1204 A.D.)

In her present life, the former *Nefertere/Queen Eleanor* became a health food counselor who worked for many years as an

---

broadcasts, and the syncronicity involved, is an example of the magnetic attraction hidden in karmic history. This is also an example of a collective repetition compulsion.

assistant vendor in the vitamin/health food section of a super-market. In a non-medical, unofficial capacity she freely advised anyone who asked about health supplements. In this way, she could work personally with the spiritual needs of hundreds of people. Her need for social stimulus was great and she possessed a natural desire to teach. A humble person (although somewhat opinionated), intellectually bright and spiritually sensitive, she developed a natural form of clairvoyance that she used to give advice to others on issues of health and life. One might say she was an early New Age worker. She was not a licensed medical practitioner and was an outspoken heretic with regard to the legal/medical establishment.

In the late 1950s and early 1960s, the former *Nefertere/Queen Eleanor* was an avid student of the work of Edgar Cayce and the Association for Research and Enlightenment (A.R.E.), located in Virginia Beach, Virginia.[24] One of the highlights of her present-day life came in the early 1960s when she was invited to give a presentation at Stanford University, in California, on the life and teachings of Edgar Cayce and the A.R.E. She accepted, believing it would be a small classroom presentation. She discovered a natural reservoir of strength deep within herself, moments before the presentation, when she realized she would be speaking in a large auditorium before an audience of over five hundred university students and professors. Totally untrained for such an experience, she found it came to her naturally. Not destined in this life for karmic fame, she dedicated herself to God, her family and her spiritual studies, and continued to work on karmic issues while she followed a path of New Age learning. At this writing, she is an elderly woman living out a quiet, anonymous life, still occasionally working on a part-time basis in a health food store. This life has offered her an opportunity to receive two great gifts: humility and simplicity.

---

[24] The A.R.E. is a well-known source of research on psychic science, past lives, natural health products and techniques, as well as higher spiritual teachings.

El Cid
Romantic Soldier and Actor

Many of Hollywood's leading men have had former lives as romanticized hero soldiers. A certain public charisma attaches itself to such warriors, whether they were, in reality, opportunists, soldiers-of-fortune or true heroes.

One such former soldier-hero has become the well-known Hollywood actor, *Charlie Sheen*, who presently lives in Los Angeles. Because his father is also a famous actor, it is easy to conclude that his destiny for this life was to become famous by offering a career in big screen movies. As a student of karmic history, you must apply a degree of detachment, spiritual insight and understanding in order to see the amazing, almost humorous, nature of this progression. We will begin by first presenting his last life as the celebrated, infamous, revolutionary hero, and former president of Mexico, *Pancho Villa*.

127

Francisco (Pancho) Villa, Doroteo Arango
(1877—1923)

Pancho Villa's given name at birth was *Doroteo Arango*. As a young man, he rejected the peonage of his parents, declared his freedom and joined an outlaw gang. During the Mexican Revolution of 1910 to 1911, he became famous for his daring and courage as a leader of the revolutionary cause. When Mexico's first revolutionary government was overthrown in 1915, *Pancho Villa*, hero of the North and head of the popular army, together with his ally Emiliano Zapata from the south of Mexico, converged on Mexico City and "liberated" it, restoring the Constitutional Party to power. For a time, *Villa* claimed the presidency, but he was later rejected. His audacious, even rash, military exploits and his populist attitude gave rise to the *Villa* myth, sung in popular ballads to this day.

What is important to our study is the fact that *Villa* so loved publicity, and the image of the dashing hero, that he surrounded himself with journalists, photographers and, in later years, film makers. He even restaged an early morning cavalry attack on a small city for a news film crew because the light at early dawn had not been good enough to capture the original action.

Pancho Villa saw himself as a popular hero and wanted to become a movie star. It is no wonder that hero magnetism has clung to him. Although a son of peasants in that life in Mexico, in a former life he was a dashing Spanish knight of privileged birth. We find this soul to be a reincarnation of the romantic Spanish cavalier known to history as Cid Campeodor (Lord Conqueror) or *El Cid*. His given name in that life was *Ruy Diaz de Vivar*. A study of his life clearly demonstrates a complex karma connected to *Villa*.

128

El Cid Campeador
(1043—1099)

Charlie Sheen
(Sept. 3, 1965—)

As the Castillian warrior *Diaz de Vivar*, this soul exhibited many of the character traits we find in *Pancho Villa*. He was loyal to a group of friends and supporters, but would not serve the dominant powers. As *El Cid,* he abandoned the Spanish cause and sided with the Moors. In time, he fought against both Moors and Castillians. His story has been elevated to classical mythic proportions. Loved by millions, even if it is only his story they love, he has karmic magnetism. Such a soul is blessed by grace that functions in a similar way to the influence of prayer. With so much popular charisma, or karmic magnetism, a subsequent career in Hollywood is not surprising. In his present life, he has become the movie actor *Charlie Sheen.*

Bruce Lee
Another Media Superstar

To fully appreciate this study, you need to research the biography of *General Robert E. Lee*, commander of the combined armies of the South during the American Civil War. Although recognized as one of the most competent and respected generals of the war, *Lee* was forced to surrender to General Grant at the Appomattox Courthouse in 1865. A collapse of further resistance and the fall of the Southern cause followed *Lee's* surrender. In reviewing *Lee's* life, you should note the glory and honor received by this relatively impoverished military genius.

Robert E. Lee was the son of General Henry Lee, a hero of the American Revolution who married a granddaughter of Martha Custis Washington—wife of George Washington, first president of the United States—from her first marriage.

General Robert E. Lee
(Jan. 19, 1807—Oct. 12, 1870)

Actor Bruce Lee
(1940—1973)

After the American Civil War and a humbling defeat, *Robert E. Lee* became the president of Washington College (now Washington and Lee University) in Lexington, Virginia. Having accepted the results of the war, he devoted the rest of his life to education and to rebuilding the South.

We find this soul entering life again outside of the United States, perhaps as a karmic consequence of having supported a movement to separate from the United States. We find him growing up in poverty, on the streets of Hong Kong, where his martial spirit and natural leadership ability led him to the discipline of karate. In this twentieth century life, he became a highly respected teacher of martial arts. In his early youth, taking advantage of a natural charisma, he was also an actor in low-budget, high-action, Hong Kong karate movies. This eventually brought him to the attention of the public worldwide.

The life story of *Bruce Lee* is a phenomenon in itself. When he first visited Hollywood, he so impressed an influential guest at a party with his display of martial arts that he was immediately offered an important role in a major Hollywood action movie. *Lee* made the jump to the Hollywood big-screen industry with amazing ease. He hardly needed to knock on the door; it opened wide upon his approach. We see karmic charisma at the root of this; being good at karate was not enough. The life and heroism of *Robert E. Lee*, already in the minds and hearts of millions of fans—including the general's picture in millions of books and on microfilm and in media archives around the world—created a huge magnetic pull for *Bruce Lee*. At an unconscious level, the general public knows who is who.

131

Bruce Lee became obsessed with the image of the undefeated hero; it was an archetype, but *Lee* choose to make it personal. This obsession, and his intense work to perfect his martial art skills, probably contributed to his early demise from a brain aneurysm. One day, at a youthful age, he simply dropped dead. It is likely that he was influencing millions to take a martial direction that no longer had true karmic worth for his own soul. His personality became stuck in a cult-hero compulsion from which he could make little spiritual progress. Therefore, his soul was called out of earth incarnation.

So where does he go next? We don't know, of course, but can we speculate? Or should we even try? One question could be this: will he be drawn deeper into the Chinese milieu, to further influence an emerging Chinese culture, or will he return to the American collective? We see that this soul had an earlier incarnation in France as a military commander in the seventeenth century. In that life, we see an example of a common French/Chinese karmic overlap. He does not, however, have a former Moslem connection, as do several other American Civil War heroes who reincarnated deeper into mainland China. It is interesting to note that mainland China is "scheduled" prophetically to become a world cradle for Christian populist democracy. This soul may serve in that movement. What effect having *Bruce Lee's* movie image shown to people on the big screen, every minute of every day around the globe, might have is unknown. We speculate that the effect on this soul's destiny will be karmically immense.

Walt Disney
French Connection

Artist, entertainment genius and entrepreneur *Walt Disney*, founder of the Disneyland empire, has an interesting past-life history. The connection between these three lives should become apparent to anyone upon study of the various biographies. This soul is an older soul, an initiate on the ray of the arts.[25]

Walt Disney, an innovator and leader in the field of film animation, had a life in the nineteenth century, as the French poet, novelist and literary personality, *Theophile Gautier*. Before that, in the seventeenth century, he was another French writer, poet and fairy tale advocate, *Charles Perrault*. All three of these lives were very public.

In 1697, French poet *Charles Perrault* wrote a collection of fairy tales entitled *Tales of Olden Times*, in which he gave classical form to the old stories of Bluebeard, Sleeping Beauty, Cinderella, Puss in Boots, Little Red Riding Hood and Hop-o-

---

[25] Essentially, there are seven basic rays or spiritual energies. They are: first, the ray of *leadership*; second, the ray of *wisdom*, education and teaching; third, the ray of *philosophy*, of synthesis of thought and universal knowledge; fourth, the ray of the *arts*, of the expression of life creation, beauty and harmony; fifth, the ray of *science*, of expression and use of primary energy; sixth, the ray of *devotion*, of loyalty, love, communion, healing and religion; and seventh, the ray of *universal union*, higher synthesis, music, ritual and white magic—combining elements of all the rays. Each of the rays has a specific color and spiritual function. A seven-candle menorah is symbolic of this esoteric principle. It is taught, as an esoteric principle, that each individual soul evolves on a ray. Every soul, through reincarnational activity, can experience any of the other rays as sub-rays. Thus, we may refer to one's main ray (the ray of one's soul's destiny), and one's sub-ray (the ray of any particular personality). One's main ray never changes. All of the rays are spiritually equal. Even national and cultural groups express ray energies. Thus, it may be said, for example, that a major sub-ray of the French is that of the *Arts*. This is not difficult to see. This study gives us an example of a French contribution to the arts.

My-Thumb. He called his collection *Tales from Mother Goose*. A literary critic on the side of enlightenment, he also published an internationally famous book of poetry.

Charles Perrault   *Theophile Gautier*
(Jan. 13,1628—May 16,1703)   *(Aug. 30, 1811—Oct. 23, 1872)*

134

Gautier was the recipient of the public recognition magnetism that clung to him as a result of his earlier life. Everything he wrote, everything he did, was somehow charmed. The French public loved him. In 1869, *Gautier* commented: "I am like a little girl in *Perrault's* fairy story. I can't open my mouth without its dropping pearls and gold coins. I should prefer to vomit an occasional toad, or a mouse (if only for a change), but I can't."

In his next life, this soul was born in the United States as *Walt Disney*. Raised on a Chicago-area farm, *Disney* attended the Academy of Fine Arts in Chicago and served as an ambulance driver in France during the First World War. An innovator in the field of animation and moving pictures, his cartoon character Mickey Mouse brought him immediate success.

The history of *Disney's* rise in the entertainment industry is well-documented. Some of his credits include *Steamboat Willie*, the first animated Mickey Mouse cartoon, produced in 1928; many other early cartoons; and the first full-length animated films, *Snow White and the Seven Dwarfs*, in 1938; and *Fantasia*, in 1940.

During the Second World War, *Disney's* cartoon work was entirely war-time propaganda. This has karmic implications.

Walter Elias Disney
(Dec. 5, 1901—Dec. 15, 1966)

In the 1950s, *Walt Disney* turned to full-length non-animated movies: *Treasure Island*, an adventure film, and *The Living Desert*, a documentary. He opened a theme park, Disneyland, in Anaheim, California in 1955. Like Coney Island, in New York, Disneyland was designed as a full-time commercial amusement park. *Walt Disney* became wealthy through these enterprises.

135

A major player in Hollywood, he entered the new field of television in the early 1960s, hosting a weekly Disneyland program. It was through television that he became an American icon, and household name, in his lifetime. He was the recipient of many media awards, Emmys and Film Academy awards. His legacy continued to spread through films, and a worldwide *Disney* empire, to *Disney* World in Florida, and to *Disney* theme parks near Paris, France and Tokyo, Japan.

Only time will tell if he has "vomited a frog or mouse, or another gold coin." Superficially, at least, it seems his life has produced a little of both. *Disney* brought fun-time entertainment to millions. Did he live up to his spiritual potential? Only God knows.

Chief Sitting Bull
A Changing of the Age

This next study demonstrates an important principle. You may decide what this is, as intuition is best strengthened by its own internal process.

Two archetypal changes are occurring in the American experience. One is the changing of the age, with its uplifting of consciousness; the other is the blending of many cultural influences, expressed through the unconscious levels of spirit. We see an internal (soul) and an external (physical) change of peoples and cultures. On a practical level, we have seen the occupation of the land mass by European invaders. Souls who were formerly Native Americans have been absorbed into modern American culture in new bodies.

A continental land mass has a consciousness, with spiritual substance and meaning. Souls who contribute to the development of spiritual archetypes appropriate for a continental evolution have the choice to remain with that continental wave. This is the same for all continental and cultural groups.

What people, or cultural group, call to a reincarnating soul? This process is woven under the direction of the incarnating soul, with the aid of angels of karma. We choose our place, our people and our families, according to soul needs. You have chosen your own.

Souls of the human wave are not new to this process. Some have had more earth experience than others, but the spirit is older and wiser than the most evolved human being. There is no race at the level of the soul. Humans, as soul entities, have been reincarnating on the earth for many hundreds of thousands of years through many peoples and cultures. The older souls, those more experienced, have lived in every racial grouping, in every continental zone, in every climate.

Those peoples and cultures that have developed the karma of increased social pressure due to larger populations, and that have become successful colonizers of lands, have often been caught up in a rush to conquer the earth. However, we must be careful to reserve judgment concerning superiority. One people is not better than another, although some conditions are harder than others. The consciousness of each cultural, ethnic or racial group, and the consciousness of each continental land mass, has its own purpose in the divine scheme of things. There is an evolution of humankind, but its process is led by spirit.

Masinissa
(238—149 B.C.)

This next case begins with the life of a North African warlord, *Masinissa*, king of East Numidia, who fought in Spain for the Carthaginians against Rome. *Masinissa* was raised and educated in Carthage. He and his tribesmen fought for Carthage as a mercenary army against Rome.

In 205 B. C., *Masinissa* changed allegiances. Perhaps seeing an advantage for his tribesmen, he joined Rome against Carthage. It is noted in history that he led his horse cavalry in a decisive charge against the Carthaginian forces at Zama, the battle that ended the Second Punic War. A large territory east of Carthage was awarded by Rome to *Masinissa* and his tribesmen for their services.

Over time *Masinissa* continued to goad the reviving Carthaginians into attacking his territory. This provided Rome with the excuse it wanted for the Third Punic War—the war that destroyed Carthage. *Masinissa* did everything he could to protect and strengthen his people, including changing loyalties as a tactic of war.

He had a life, again as a war leader, among the Mongols in the time preceding the rise of Genghis Khan. In that life, this soul experienced the karma of being double-crossed by an enemy who changed loyalties. In this karmic episode, his own life, his family and his entire tribe were destroyed and their ancestral lands taken.

We find him again entering the stream of history as an American colonial officer who became a hero of the American Revolution, *General Anthony Wayne*.

General "Mad Anthony" Wayne
(Jan. 1, 1745—Dec. 15, 1796)

The biography of *General Anthony Wayne* is revealing. Called *"Mad Anthony"* (due, perhaps, to his impetuous, hot-headed nature), he was a brave and competent officer in battle. This is another example of the rise of talent from the ranks of ordinary people—if we dare consider anyone "ordinary."

Wayne was a surveyor and farmer before joining in the organized resistance to British rule. As we have seen, the British of that time were a Roman-group reincarnation. Some of the American Colonists were former Carthaginians. For example, another organizer of resistance to British rule in the American Colonies at that time, although not directly associated with *Wayne*, was Ethan Allen. Allen was a reincarnation of Hannibal, the Carthaginian General who was finally defeated by Rome at the battle of Zama, in 206 B.C. *Masinissa* had deserted the

Carthaginians, and the cause of Hannibal and his brothers, to fight for Rome; thus, we see a karmic loop. Loyalty, however, was not a problem in the life of *Anthony Wayne*.

After the Revolutionary War, *Wayne* continued with the United States Army, fighting in the wars of Indian settlement in the Northwest Territories. The Indians, who had been allied with the British during the Revolutionary War, were defeated and treaties were made. These first agreements between the United States and the native tribes ceded lands to the Indians.

General Anthony Wayne made promises to the Indians that these treaties would be honored. He lived to see them dishonored. Since he had pledged his truthfulness, he took this to be a personal dishonor. It is likely that he had learned a hard karmic lesson in his life as a Mongol chieftain concerning the destructiveness of disloyalty as a tactic of politics and war. *Wayne* did not wish to be party to deceitful negotiations or to false treaty settlements. By the time he died, he was filled with anger about U.S. treachery toward the Indian nations. This may explain his Native American reincarnation forty years later, as a member of the Hunkpapa Sioux nation. This soul became known to history as *Chief Sitting Bull*.

139

Sioux Chief Sitting Bull
(1834—1890)

Evolving on the first-ray path of organizational leadership, this Sioux soldier soul demonstrated unusual charisma and power from an early age. He quickly rose to a position of leadership and respect among his people. He was also considered a seer and medicine man (*medicine* meaning spirit power). This soul may indeed have been on a spiritual mission to help the people of the Sioux nation.

A karmic link from North Africa extended to the Native American people of that era. In the Sioux nation, we find a mass reincarnation of the East Numidians of North Africa from the time of *Masinissa.* A half a century earlier, the Sioux were allied with the British (partially former Romans) against the American Colonists (partially former Carthaginians). This was a time of karmic choices and repetitions. An irreversible course of events was to be played out.

The Sioux people—actually several tribal subgroups—had been driven out of the Northeast Territories a hundred and fifty years earlier by a people called Ojibwa, who were armed by the French. Sioux migration had been from the Northeast, generally toward the Southwest. By the eighteenth century, the Sioux had driven out other native groups (Cheyenne and Kiowa) and had occupied the beautiful Black Hills of South Dakota. From this sacred mountainous terrain, they spread into the Northern plains. Their history of political alliances was karmic. First they sided with the British against the friends of their common enemies, the French. Then, as a result, they supported the British against the American Colonists. This was a culturally "fatal" choice.

140

After the American Revolution, the Sioux were settled by U.S. treaty in South Dakota. When gold was discovered in the Black Hills, the treaty was dishonored. Several Sioux warriors, including *Sitting Bull,* left the reservation for open land and free hunting in the West. This decision provoked hostilities with the post-Civil War U. S. (martial law) administrative government of the Western territories. Many "white eyes" (a slur used by the Indians) wanted war. Whether it was greed or a concept of manifest destiny, the Euro-Americans would not relent—much as the Romans had sought an excuse to attack Carthage.[26]

On June 25, 1876, the combined Indian forces of several thousand warriors destroyed the main body of the U.S. 7th Cavalry at

---

[26] These are karmic circles within circles. The East Numidian tribesmen played a karmic role in provoking Carthage to its eventual, and total, destruction.

the battle of the Little Big Horn. General Armstrong Custer, a hero of the American Civil War—and a former pre-Alexandrian Persian military officer—who was commanding the 7th Cavalry, was killed at this time. It was—no matter how glorified by some— a hopeless rebellion. *Sitting Bull*, contrary to popular history, did not take part directly in the battle of the Little Big Horn.

Sitting Bull was later chosen to represent his people at a treaty settlement council held with the U.S. Territorial (military) administration. *Sitting Bull* was greatly disappointed by the settlement that the combined tribes were willing to accept. One of the first Indian representatives to leave the treaty council, the aging Chief was surrounded by reporters. One newsman asked him, "What have the Indians decided?" *Sitting Bull's* sarcastic remark, "There are no more Indians!" can be interpreted as prophecy.

In later years, *Sitting Bull* joined Buffalo Bill Cody's Wild West Show. With a mounted entourage of Indian braves in full battle regalia, he rode around the circus ring, whooping and having fun. He watched as thousands of paid customers came from around the world to see the Indian braves and the famous Indian Chief.

Toward the end of his life, *Sitting Bull's* personality grew more sullen, settling into a depression. A dark cloud of dissatisfaction is visible in photographs of the aging warrior. During this period, he began to rail, with increasing sarcasm, against white persecution and the unfair losses of the past. He sank into, and seemed to become overwhelmed by, the psychic experience of the Hunkpapa Sioux. He joined an Indian religious movement, then on the rise, called the "Ghost Dance." Evangelistic in nature, the Ghost Dance carried a group hypnotic prayer that the world would revert to the past. According to the Ghost Dance vision, the white man would be gone, the buffalo would return and the old people would repopulate the earth. A religion born of despair, the Ghost Dance enhanced group togetherness, yet it appealed to hopelessness.

As a Native American Chief, *Sitting Bull* is still placed on a pedestal. Many people, especially Native Americans, consider him an icon of resolute Indian spiritual power. The deeper truth of this exists in that part of his life experience that best expresses spiritual release from past karma. *Sitting Bull* withdrew into a personality shell at the end of his life; those who place this phase of his life on a pedestal of exemplary leadership are choosing to honor a retrograde expectation, and an angry, unenlightened truculence.

Sitting Bull reincarnated, in a very short time, in the United States to Caucasian parents, perhaps drawing on the karmic connection of this life as a hero of the American Revolution. Rapid reincarnation can be seen in many lives with dissatisfied endings. Quick reincarnation is common when the sense of "being undone" is powerful. The Ghost Dance would have contributed to a strong emotional desire for resurrection in new life, although that was not its expressed purpose. The soul of *Sitting Bull* made it big in Hollywood as the movie actor *John Wayne*.

142

John (the "Duke") Wayne
(May 26, 1907—June 11, 1979)

Born *Marion Michael Morrison* in Winterset, Iowa, *John Wayne* went on to become one of Hollywood's biggest stars, appearing in over a hundred movies. At the age of seventeen, he left home and made his way to Los Angeles, where he attended school. Recall that *Masinissa* was sent by his father, the king, to be raised and educated in Carthage. Perhaps remembering the excitement of the Wild West Show, or perhaps guided by a guardian angel, he was unconsciously drawn to Hollywood and the center of the new film entertainment industry. Old photos of *Sitting Bull*, portraits and biographies of *Anthony Wayne*, even historical records of *Masinissa*, contributed to this soul's magnetic pull toward fame.

In Los Angeles in 1934, during the Great Depression, *Wayne* lived on small jobs, finally finding work with a movie company. He did anything to stay around the sets, including sweeping the stables and taking care of the horses. Eventually he landed bit parts as an "extra." He was a tall, good-looking young man, with an amazing natural charisma. He wasn't a particularly good actor; however, when he finally got a chance to play a small speaking part as a cowboy, the director noticed him. He had something special.

Wayne's early film persona epitomized the archetypal American frontiersman. He won an Academy Award for his work in *True Grit,* in which he played the caricature of a crusty old Western he-man cowboy. The rest of the story is film history.

John Wayne is still a popular folk hero. His acting persona exemplified the myth of the noble, undefeated, big-hearted, hard-edged, relentless in enmity (yet generous toward the defeated), pioneering spirit. It is interesting that *Wayne* played the role of Genghis Khan. This archetypal role exemplified what is loved and honored in the American pioneer myth, as well as the Mongol and Native American myths: the generous, faithful, tough-guy hero, who would protect his family and give his life for a friend.

The past-life history of *John Wayne* demonstrates the melting pot of America. The consciousness of "middle" America expresses both the best and the less-than-best of many cultures, including that of the Mongol and Native American. The rise and fall of the Indian nations has been highly mythologized. The karma of these groups is perfectly merged in present-day reality. As one Navajo mystic recently said, "Those souls who are trapped on reservations in Indian bodies are not former Indians; they are the people who built the reservations to keep the Indians there." Although this Navajo mystic, who believes in reincarnation, meant this with an element of sardonic humor, there is truth in his sentiment. Most of the souls of early Native Americans have moved on according to their personal karma.

143

The souls of former Indians who lived good lives, cared for their families, cherished freedom and honored the spirit of the land are still in the Americas. Such former Indians have reincarnated throughout western America. For example, many of these souls have embraced such cultural forms as American country western music, the center of which is in the beautiful hills of Branson, Missouri. This area was a sacred power center— a "medicine" center—for earlier Native American peoples. Thus, it may be said that American country western music, as an art form, was strongly influenced by the "rise again" of the Indian nations: the Cheyenne, the Cherokee, the Seminole and many others, reincarnating in middle American culture.

We may ask, "From what past-life cultural influence do country western stars such as Willie Nelson, Loretta Lynn, Pasty Cline or Garth Brooks get their characteristic ways?" In former lives, they had names such as *Black Elk* and *Singing Bird*. In their present lives, these white folks are often called *red necks* in popular slang. Country western is *red-neck* music. Even those country western performers who happen to be of African American or Asian heritage don't seem to mind the "red neck" label, frequently making fun of it.

144

Howard R. Hughes
The "Marmluks" of Nevada

This case may test the resilience of your acceptance. The age of *Genghis Khan* and the Mongol conquests, which began in the late twelfth century and continued into the thirteenth century, is recorded in Western biography in mostly negative terms. We must shake off that negative perspective in order to see a deeper cultural mutation, and karma, at work.

Hulagu Khan
(1217—1265)

Hulagu Khan, a grandson of Genghis Khan, conquered all of Persia in the thirteenth century. He can be connected with several past lives as an aristocratic warrior: as a noble warlord in Persia, around 300 B.C.; in Egypt, around 1700 B.C.; and before that, around 3500 B.C., as a nobleman in the early Aryan conquests of Afghanistan, Pakistan, India and Persia. During the period under King Hammurabbi, he experienced a life as a minor prince of old Babylon.[27]

Hulagu is remembered as the warlord who wiped out the notorious Assassin sect of Persia in 1256, a group that plagued the Middle

---

[27] Ham-mu-rabbi roughly translates as *servant and revealer* of "I AM" ("Ham" meaning "I Am," "mu" meaning "revelation," "rabbi" meaning "spiritual teacher"). Therefore, Hammurabbi is an early archetype of "Moses"—carver in stone of the law of the solar deity "I AM." It may

East, and even parts of Europe, with organized crime, kidnapping, extortion and assassinations for hire. His forces took Baghdad in 1258, ending the Abbasid empire. He took Aleppo in 1260, but his force was eventually checked by the Marmluk (or Mameluke) people, a former slave-soldier society that ruled Egypt and its surrounding territories through a militant Moslem social order.

Hulagu worked out a compromise that embraced the Moslem faith. He then withdrew to the East and established the first non-Arab Moslem Khanate, which included all of Persia. This was the seed of what became the Mogul empire, a Moslem order that eventually, after *Hulagu's* death, spread further east to conquer northern India.

The karmic roots of these military conquests are connected to earlier ages. Genghis Khan was the former Alexander the Great. Although they may appear different when perceived through Western eyes, the characters, and even goals, of *Genghis Khan* and *Alexander* were similar.

We must look on the lives of former warlords with detachment and compassion. Perhaps they did not know what they were doing. Or, perhaps they were doing what they were supposed to be doing—at that time in history. Or, perhaps what they did, after the "changing of the age," with the coming of Christ, was a form of compulsive repetition. Perhaps such warlords needed the influence of more enlightened teachings to show them a way toward peace. As Jesus said, "Judge not least you be judged, for all have fallen short of the Glory of God."

146

In any case, *Hulagu Khan* was continuing in the karmic path of an effective warrior and conqueror. His compromise with the Marmluks, and his acceptance of the Moslem faith as an um-

---

take some inner work to comprehend the meaning of this. One of the primal spiritual archetypes of soldier souls such as Hammurabbi and his officers, would have been the admonition from a higher spiritual impulse to "go forth and conquer (make order) in the world." Like his later incarnation as King Ashoka of India (another carrier of "Moses" spiritual energy), Hammurabbi was a soldier king who embraced religion and religious reform and who, like Moses, carved "God's and the nations' laws in stone.

brella for his Khanate, indicate that he was much more than an indiscriminate destroyer. In this case, perhaps the courage and conviction of the Moslem soldier society of the Marmluks represented the influence of a more enlightened teaching.

Among other things, *Hulagu Khan* was an intellectual genius. He was also a recluse and a dreamer of future empires. As was common to his culture, he kept a harem, collecting women as token playthings. Nevertheless, or perhaps because of this, he lived as a lonely exile; although a king, he was always a "stranger in a strange land." After his death and the collapse of his empire, the Marmluks took over most of *Hulagu's* western lands and continued to rule them for a quarter millennia. A reincarnated branch of Marmluks, the American Mormons, repeated this karmic inheritance in a later incarnation in Nevada.

A deep biographical search is recommended in order to prepare one to more easily accept this soul's eventual progression into twentieth century America. Born to a wealthy family in Texas—his father owned important oil drilling patents—*Howard Hughes* expanded his family's fortune, becoming one of the wealthiest men in the world.

147

Howard R. Hughes
(Dec. 24, 1905—Apr. 5, 1976)

Howard Hughes was a businessman, war-time industrialist, dreamer, inventor, aviator, movie producer and notorious social playboy. In his later years, he became known for the mystery surrounding his person. At the age of twenty-one, he inherited

Hughes Tool Company from his father. His estimated yearly income during the Depression years of the 1930s was two million dollars—a great fortune. In addition to his many business activities, he was drawn to Hollywood.

Hughes produced several movies; among the earliest and best were *The Front Page* (1931) and the story of gangster Al Capone, *Scarface* in (1932). During this period, he collected famous Hollywood actresses, including Jane Mansfield and Marilyn Monroe, as mistresses—and as tokens of conquest. Women have said of *Hughes* that, at his best, he was every woman's dream man but, at his worse, he was distant and deceptive. The karma of having lived with a "royal harem" can carry a deep spiritual burden.

Hughes also formed a company to build experimental aircraft, Hughes Aircraft. He had a progressive psychological disability, suffering paranoid delusions about the danger of germs. This psychological affliction, inherited from an emotionally unstable mother, was enhanced by a flying accident in which he suffered severe burns over much of his body. After this accident, *Hughes* actually became vulnerable to disease, due to the fire-caused damage to his immune system. He became a recluse, and was seldom seen in public again.

It did not end there, although finding more of his biography may be difficult. Karmically speaking, he still held the credit of having destroyed the Assassin sect of Persia. In destroying this sect in its mountain fortress, *Hulagu's* forces had done what no others had been able to accomplish: not even the Western crusaders or the organized Marmluks. The Assassin sect's oath and its resultant crime energy is a karmic force that has continued to call its former participants to reincarnate in various parts of the world. (Look at its impact on Russia today.)

As a basic principle, crime energy—especially among those groups that take dark oaths, swearing on blood and blade—will continue to reincarnate. Souls who have served such groups, who have taken an oath to profit at the expense of others at the point of the sword, or who advocate superstition or immorality in the name of God, and who have not repented or repudiated the energy of their dark oaths, are called to reenact those former lives until they choose to change their promises. In the Bible, Jesus said, "Do not make oaths. Make your answers yes or no, for no one knows where the Spirit may lead tomorrow."

Howard Hughes made the movie *Scarface* in 1932. In so doing, he was dealing with the crime energy of gangster Al Capone. In a former incarnation, Al Capone was a Roman governor of Judea around 70 A.D., under Vespasian (who became J. Edgar Hoover) and Titus (who became FBI enforcer Eliot Ness). In making that movie, *Hughes* attracted a karmic energy that cast him against a group of reincarnating Assassins from 1300 A.D.

Some of the former Siccari[28] incarnated to become involved in crime activity in the United States. In the late 1920s and early 1930s, one of the lieutenants of one of these organized crime families from New Jersey, by the name of "Bugsy" Segal, was assigned to Los Angeles as overlord of "family" operations. Like

---

[28] In 70 A.D., a group of Judean Zealots, called "Siccari" (meaning *blades*) was active in the resistance to Vespasian and the Roman legion. Some of this group were directly responsible for the destruction of the temple in Jerusalem in 70 A.D. Having forcibly occupied the temple, under the objections of the orthodox, minions of these Siccari went out and cut the throats of several sleeping Roman soldiers. As a result, the Roman legion, against the orders of their commanders, sacked the temple where the offending Zealots were hiding. Some of these Siccari reincarnated into the Moslem sect of the Assassins, a thousand years later. In recent history, we have seen a reoccurrence of this violation as a small branch of reincarnated Siccari (with their repeated "blood-sword" militant oaths-to-the-death, against the objections of the Orthodox) stormed and held the Holy Sikh temple at Amritsar on the Pakistan/India border. We saw a similar repetition incarnated in World War II in the German militant SS cult.

It cannot be emphasized too strongly: those who have embraced the sword with religious blood oaths, without repentance, are led by that karma to reincarnate in world zones of violent conflict. Social disorder provides karmic opportunity for expression of former criminal promises. Unrepentant, reincarnated crime-cult oath members may be at the height of their karmic dark path when they become representatives of official government. This becomes a problem for everyone. As is normal with other less destructive cases, such karmically challenged souls often reincarnate with former partners; this is how former crime families, and criminal or opportunistic political movements, evolve forward in time.

149

Hughes, Segal was seduced by Hollywood and had a notorious affair with a well-known movie actress. Perhaps he met *Howard Hughes* at this time; this is unknown.[29]

How does this connect with the life of *Howard Hughes?* Segal was the "godfather" of the first major casino development in Las Vegas, Nevada. His casino was conceived as a money laundering scheme, which is how the New Jersey Mob, a major ethnic crime syndicate, came to control most of Las Vegas. This story became interesting when *Howard Hughes* decided to buy all the available land in southern Nevada, especially around Las Vegas. The former *Hulagu Khan* came into direct conflict with reincarnated minions of the Assassin sect.

When *Hughes* created his corporate flagship, the Summa Corporation,[30] the officers of this company were selected by *Hughes* from among those of the Mormon faith. *Hughes,* although not a Mormon, liked Mormons because they did not drink, smoke or use foul language. In *Hughes'* estimation, Mormons were stable, moral and trustworthy. With this management group, and with Summa Corporation's growing power in Nevada politics, *Hughes* helped clean up Las Vegas. The power of the Mob was broken— or, at least, it went more deeply underground. Laws were made in

For these wayward souls, who are caught in a repetition compulsion of crime, an idealistic purpose (such as "my family," or "our cause") is often used to justify a destructive means that can include methods such as social or political domination, lying, deception, extortion and murder.

As an example, we see a rise of an angry, militant religious-repressive energy in Iran today, supporting terrorist activities to neighboring states. The latest development of this type of expression of "dark karma" was spearheaded by the reincarnation in Iran, at the turn of the century, of a former "Old Man of the Mountain." Although he has since died, this "dark energy" is still promoted by his followers, who are presently in control of the Iranian government. (The "Old Man" was the name of several former leaders of the Moslem Assassin sect.) Additional study is recommended.

[29] There is a famous Hollywood movie about this gangster's life, entitled *Bugsy.*

[30] Even this name has some unconscious significance and linkage through the Latin, to ancient Persia and India.

Nevada that no person with any organized-crime connections could directly own interest in a Nevada casino.

In his plan for a future empire, *Hughes* had envisioned the creation of the world's largest airport outside Las Vegas. His plans included a world-class transportation hub to serve the American Southwest with commuter planes and high-speed magnetic trains providing access to all the Western states. Summa Corporation would control all the open land around this central commercial transportation hub. When *Hughes* died, no written will was found, and no immediate heirs. Therefore, Summa Corporation bought up all of its own stock, which allowed its Mormon management to continue to control all of Summa's assets and its future direction.

The Akashic Records suggest that many of those who are Mormons in the Western United States were formerly Moslems. Some of these were formerly of the Marmluk soldier society in the thirteenth century.[31] A remnant branch of the Moslem Marmluk people again became the recipients of the crumbling empire of the former *Hulagu Khan.* We see a stylized version of karmic repetition over a very long cycle.

151

---

[31] Many former Native Americans have been attracted to the Mormon faith; many of these were formerly Mongol and Moslem, reincarnating from the East and the Middle East.

Joseph Smith
Founder of the Mormons

The biography of *Joseph Smith*, and the story of the founding of the Mormon movement in the United States, constitutes one of the more interesting events in the history of world religion.

In the sixteenth century, the Dutch Anabaptists established what they referred to as the "kingdom of Munster" (Munster is a town in Germany). They were radical Protestant reformers who vowed to establish a new theocracy. In 1534, the bishop of Munster had them killed during their attempt to break the occupation.

Jan Matthijs   *Joseph Smith*
(c. 1505—April 5, 1534)   *(Dec. 23, 1805—June, 27, 1844)*

Joseph Smith was a reincarnation of *Johann Matthijs*. *Joseph Smith's* brother Hyrum was the former Jan Beuckelszoon, better known as Jan van Leiden, who lived around 1509 to 1536. The militant Anabaptist Bernd Knipperdolling, who led the original coup to control of the city of Munster, also reincarnated in Mormon history. He became Brigham Young, who, after the death of the first "prophet," *Joseph Smith*, led the Mormons out of the United States, away from persecution, into what was then Mexico—the Great Salt Lake, which is now Salt Lake City, Utah.

At the age of seventeen, *Joseph Smith* had a vision revealing the existence of secret records. Five years later, he reported that he had found golden tablets inscribed with secret writings. No one ever saw these tablets, but *Smith* dictated them to others who transcribed them. The result was the *Book of Mormon*.

Jailed in Carthage, Illinois, on arson charges, *Joseph Smith* and his brother Hyrum were shot and killed by an angry mob. They were being held on charges of ordering the destruction of a newspaper that had vilified them. *Joseph Smith's* political, social and religious activism had alienated him from his neighbors.

In 1844, *Joseph Smith's* life was taken by an act of violence; he reincarnated in China in 1875.

Charles Jones Soong—Soong Yau Ju
(1875—May 3, 1918)

153

Born to impoverished parents on South China's Hainan Island, *Yau Ju Soong* was adopted by an "uncle" and taken to Boston, Massachusetts to labor in a tea and silk shop. The boy, wanting an education, ran away.

Yau Ju Soong, speaking little English, was accepted as a ship's boy by Captain Gabrialson, who was master of the Bostonian ship on which *Soong* had stowed away. Gabrialson introduced "Charlie," as they called him, to evangelical religion. *Soong*, who was called at different times "Sun" and "Soon," was eventually baptized *Charles Jones Soong*. Converting to Protestant evangelical Christianity, he completed his education in the United

States. After years of preparation in American fundamentalist Bible culture, *Charles Soong* returned to China to become a Methodist missionary and political activist.

Soong became a multi-millionaire as a merchant, due in part to his adoptive American father, tobacco magnate Julian S. Carr, of Durham, North Carolina. Back in China *Soong* married the daughter of the head of one of China's most powerful Tongs. The *Soong* family's influence on modern China amounts to that of a dynasty. In fact, there is a connection to the Soong, or Sung, Dynasty of the twelfth century. The *Soong* family biography is really quite amazing.[32]

One of *Soong's* daughters married Chang Kai-Shek, general of the nationalist Chinese government; another married Chinese revolutionary Dr. Sun Yat Sen, called by many "Father of the Revolution." Another daughter married H. H. Kung, former finance minister of the nationalist government. This extended family line became a major financial force in New York, San Francisco and Dallas, Texas.

Soong's three biological sons are among the richest people in the world. T.V. Soong, prime minister of nationalist China for a while, became a billionaire by taking advantage of an artificially controlled government currency exchange rate. Before, during and after World War II, T.V. Soong converted U.S. foreign aid money and Christian missionary, charitable contributions, primarily from the United States, into millions of dollars on the Chinese foreign currency black market—at a profit as high as 2000:1. *Charlie Soong's* other two sons, T. L. and T. A. Soong, began family financial dynasties in New York and San Francisco, respectively.

154

Although we will not engage in investigative criminal research, it appears that *Charlie Soong* was murdered, probably by a slow-working poison. This soul reincarnated in Korea, in 1920, as *Sun Myung Moon.*

---

[32] For more information, see *The Soong Sisters,* by Emily Hahn, 1941 and 1970, or *The Soong Dynasty,* by Sterling Seagrave, 1985.

The Reverend Sun Myung Moon
(Jan. 6, 1920—)

Founder of the Unification Church, with over three million followers worldwide, the *Reverend Sun Myung Moon* claims to be a perfect messenger from God. He has been quoted as saying, "I am the Buddha, I am Confucius, I am Jesus, I am Mohammed." He has taught that he himself has the possibility of becoming the true Messiah. And many believe.

Friedrich Hegel

A Master Sophist

This study is about intellectual discrimination on the path of spiritual learning. All our assumptions deserve constant review. We must strive to be conscious of the fine impulse of intuitive guidance that is higher than intellect and to be conscious of what influences us in the process of intellectual development. Much of what we do in life is greatly influenced by unconscious assumptions. Whom do we believe? Whom do we follow? Whom do we allow to influence our minds? Such influences affect our feelings and beliefs. What we believe, whether right or wrong, is highly karmic.

In this study, the issue is spiritual pretense masquerading as intellectual authority. Intellectual authoritarianism does not enhance, and can even defeat, true spiritual guidance.

There is great substance to *Gorgias'* biography, although not much from antiquity is still available. In his works *On Not-Being,* or *On Nature, Gorgias* stipulated that (1) nothing exists; (2) if anything exists, it cannot be known and (3) if it can be known, it cannot be communicated to others.

Gorgias of Leontini (Sicily)   *Georg Wilhelm Friedrich Hegel*
(483—376 B.C.)   *(Aug. 27, 1770—Nov. 14, 1831)*

The Greek philosopher Plato wrote a treatise entitled *Gorgias,* in which he chronicled a debate between *Gorgias* and the Athenian philosopher Socrates. Perceiving Socrates to have more wisdom than *Gorgias*, who was widely considered to be a master of the skills of argument and persuasion, a student asked Socrates, "What is the difference between you and the sophists?"

"I know that I know not, and they know not that they know not," was Socrates' response. This cryptic answer instructed the student on a delicate issue in the pursuit of truth. Namely, that the pursuit of truth can be ignored, befuddled or defeated by false wisdom cloaked in intellectual sophistry.

Georg Hegel was a German idealist philosopher whose thought greatly influenced modern philosophy. He was, for a while, a professor at the University of Jena, then professor at Heidelberg and later, until his death in 1831, at Berlin. His mentality was probably appreciated by more students—and with less discrimination—than any other European philosopher in history. Part of this love affair with *Hegel* among young intellectuals may be due to a fascination with the sheer volume of his thought, as well as his subtle artistry with words, with which he concealed spiritual emptiness.

Sir Julian Huxley, the famous British naturalist and biologist, once commented about *Hegel's* thought, "Conversancy with *Hegel* is sufficient to deprave the mind." Huxley, it seems, was unable to find, or unwilling to keep searching for, a straight and true path in *Hegel's* work. Huxley's mind was strong enough not to be fascinated or confused by *Hegel's* potent linguistic artistry.

157

This was not the case for many thousands of Hegelian disciples who have been drawn to the knee of this master of *"spiritual nihilism."* This included, in a twisted and complex way, young intellectuals such as Karl Marx, who tried to "out-Hegel" *Hegel*. From an impersonal review of the spiritual condition of *Hegel's* personality, it is possible to conclude that he suffered from a form of spiritual distortion. This condition of being stuck in a space of potent, but spiritually empty, intellectuality (a type of mind-soul separation) has continued for thousands of years through many of his incarnations.

Sir Francis Bacon
... And the Theosophical Society

The following study presents insights into the progress of a great soul. This former fourth-degree initiate has become a spiritual master, having taken the fifth degree of initiation. In the persona of an Indian (Kashmiri) master of wisdom, he created a role for himself in the creation of the nineteenth century Theosophical Society as one of the mysterious masters of the society. Thus, the origin of the Theosophical Society was indeed sponsored by true spiritual masters. However, in some ways, the creation of the Society was also a world-class dramatic act, a kind of educational "passion play." When we read about the cast of characters in early theosophy, a great deal of light is shed on this fascinating chapter in the history of world religion, philosophy and education.

The full potency of a great soul is not fully manifest in any of their personalities expressed on earth. A great soul, one who is not yet a spiritual master, is like a socially magnetic "transformer" whose efforts can affect the karma of a whole people. These souls set the tempo of learning according to their successes and their failures. Through spiritual courage and faith in God, they have the potential to uplift the entire collective with whom they have incarnated.

A great soul is rare; a spiritual master is even more rare. The earth has thus far produced only a couple hundred or so true spiritual masters. This study focuses on the past lives of one of these.

Sir Francis Bacon was one of the great universal geniuses of all time; a proper study will help you grasp the potency of this soul's inner development. He was not a spiritual master in that life—but he was a great soul. Spiritual mastery, which is "not of this earth," came to this great soul later, after yet another life, in an incarnation in upper India in the 1700s. In that life, he was a prince among the Sikh people of Kashmir.

But what of the life of *Sir Francis Bacon*? Was *Bacon's* full arhat potential active in that life? This is a difficult question. The answer can be understood by focusing on the degree of multidimensional genius that *Bacon* expressed on many levels of his persona. Although the fact has been bitterly debated over the centuries, it is true that he was the primary literary genius behind the plays of William Shakespeare. *Bacon* is considered by many to be the father of the modern scientific method. He was a genius of rational thought and a great philosophic synthesizer, as well as a political activist. Although he was born to this calling, politics later brought about his personal downfall.

Francis Bacon
(Jan. 22, 1561—Apr. 9, 1626)

In one of the volumes of *Wisdom*, published by the Wisdom Society for the Advancement of Knowledge, Learning and Research in Education in the 1960s, Loren Eiseley wrote of *Sir Francis Bacon*:

In January of 1561 a son was born to Nicholas Bacon, Lord Keeper to Elizabeth I. In twelve years this bright, grave child, Francis, would be called by Elizabeth her little Lord Keeper, but all his life she would deny him great office (as one denies, yet counsels with, a wizard), and all his life poverty and ill fortune would dog him in the midst of luxury. Yet it is this man who first fully visualized in all its splendor the "invention of inventions"— the experimental method which would unlock the riches of the modern world.

Sir Francis Bacon's life bridges the cultural gulf between the end of monarchy and the birth of the modern world. He served the court of King James I as Lord Chancellor, following in his father's footsteps of royal service. Set up and trapped by vindictive enemies at court, *Bacon* was accused of taking bribes. Rather than practice common sense self-protection, as such political intrigue would require, *Bacon* relied on promises from King James. *Bacon* settled the political attack by admitting he had received what was "traditional homage." He is quoted as saying, "I am the sacrifice. I hope that I will be the last." Essentially, James I, the proud, self-serving sponsor of the King James Bible, threw *Bacon* to the wolves to save himself and the reputation of his court.

Who had *Sir Francis Bacon* been in other lives? At the age of twelve, he entered Trinity College, in Cambridge. He developed skills at the level of genius in at least three different directions simultaneously—almost as if three separate personalities were struggling to come out.

First and most potent among his past personas was the thirteenth century British Franciscan monk *Roger Bacon*. It is from this incarnation that this future spiritual master has been wrongly identified by some theosophists as Saint Francis of Assisi. *Roger Bacon* was a Franciscan monk, but with a different soul path than Saint Francis.

Roger Bacon
(c. 1220—1292)

A student who has not yet done a comprehensive study of the life of *Roger Bacon* is in for a surprise, and an adventure of discovery. He was one of the most interesting teachers and philosophers of that most interesting of centuries, the thirteenth.

The psychospiritual energy of the thirteenth century A.D. was a progression and upgrade of the thirteenth century B.C. These two centuries stand at critical cultural transformation points in their respective ages. Both of these thirteenth century periods—A.D. and B.C.—were times of great psychological and spiritual transformation.

England in the thirteenth century A.D. was a karmic reflection of Egypt in the thirteenth century B.C. These two places, times and "socio-karmic complexes" involved collective incarnations that underwent parallel spiritual evolution over a two thousand year period. Christianity has roots in the Amarna period of ancient Egypt and, to a lesser extent, in the temple of *On* (Heliopolis), where Joseph and Mary are said to have taken Jesus for his first few years. *Roger Bacon* was a transformative personality from the Egyptian period of the Amarna enlightenment.

Buried deeply in the karmic past of *Bacon's* soul were two lives lived in rapid succession in ancient Greece around 485 B.C. One was as one of the most talented playwrights of old Athens, *Sophocles*. The other, a life shortly before *Sophocles,* was as an elder in the school of Pythagoras who was killed during a mob attack.[33] The life as the Pythagorean elder was most directly related to the life of *Roger Bacon*—in its genius as teacher, recluse, mystic and monk. The next life, as *Sophocles* was the most directly related, at least as far as personal karma is concerned, to *Sir Francis Bacon,* Chancellor of State.

161

Some of the surviving Pythagorean disciples became early influences in the golden age of Athenian democracy. Remnant Pythagoreans had various forms of influence on such philosophers as Anaxagoras, who became the friend and teacher of Pericles, Socrates and Alcibiades. *Sophocles* was both interested in, and influenced by, Pythagorean teaching. However, this great soul had not been Pythagoras, as some theosophists have incor-

---

[33] The school of Pythagoras was destroyed by a politically incited mob. Many of the students and teachers at the Pythagorean compound at the time of the mob attack were killed, including this elder teacher. Further study on the Pythagoreans is recommended.

rectly thought.[34] (The future lives of Socrates, Pericles, Alcibiades and Anaxagoras are discussed in a later study.)

Sophocles' service to the Athenian military is linked to his last moments on earth as the Pythagorean who died defenselessly at the hands of the unruly mob. *Roger Bacon* was a Franciscan pacifist. *Sir Francis Bacon* was a chief of the British state, which required attention to militancy, in much the same way that *Sophocles'* life demanded military responsibilities.

Sophocles
(496—406 B.C.)

162

Sophocles was born to an aristocratic family in Athens. He was a soldier and military officer, as was required of all Athenian aristocratic youth at that time. *Sophocles* eventually rose to the position of commanding general, leading the Athenian army. In this capacity, he shared power with Pericles, the famous orator and Athenian political leader around whom the golden age of Greek democracy is said to have begun.

Sophocles is considered one of the greatest Greek playwrights. He is believed to have written as many as 123 plays and won 24

---

[34] Pythagoras achieved spiritual mastery at the end of that life in 500 B.C. Although he is still an elder brother in the higher schools of wisdom, the great one that was Master Pythagoras has never returned to earth— nor is that a likely expectation. Joining Pythagoras in the great academy of the higher dimensions of the planet is as difficult now as it would have been to enter his school on earth. Some Masters require total preparation before they meet with a student. Master Pythagoras is one of these.

victories in the city's annual dramatic contests. A study of the plays of *Sophocles* demonstrates remarkable karmic overlap, even overshadowing, with respect to the life of *Sir Francis Bacon*. If one were to take the life of *Sophocles*, add the karmic potency from the emotion of his writings, shuffle it all in a deck of cards and deal it out to a future life, one could easily imagine the result in the circumstances of *Francis Bacon's* incarnation. This image of the "cards of destiny" clearly defines *Bacon's* personality—his aspirations, efforts, successes and failures. This perspective even presages *Bacon's* tragic disgrace by a self-protective, fearful king.[35]

The *Francis Bacon*/Shakespeare connection is a hotly contested controversy. We believe that *Bacon* was the primary motivating force in the writing of the Shakespearean plays. *Bacon* formed a literary/acting guild, a group with whom he met in a roadhouse inn or pub. With each assigned a part, these fellows developed *Bacon's* plays. For *Bacon*, the great word-master, it was relaxing fun. This diversion allowed one of this soul's highly potent "past personas," that of *Sophocles*, to have its needed expression. Together, this group would shake loose the muse, so to speak. "Shakespeare," as the group effort was called, touched the heart of the human condition in a way that resembled the great passion of the plays of ancient Athens.

The flow of the genius of Shakespeare was called forth by the group, but it was inspired by the mental energy of *Bacon*, without whom it never would have come into being. The actual task of writing the plays was largely done by *Bacon* himself, who transcribed the endless lines from his illumined intellect and a perfected photographic memory.

The plays were democratic, populist, heretical and distinctly anti-aristocratic. They were psychologically devastating to old royal pretensions. *Bacon* never admitted his part in the play writing pub-

---

[35] In *Sophocles'* writing we see noble and rigid, but heroic, idealism expressed in the play *Ajax*. We discover abject self-denial projected in the form of a tormented conflict between the individual's and the state's needs in his play *Antigone*. We experience the conflict of the psyche in unresolved games of human desire and ambition, and a glimpse of the naked human heart, in *Sophocles' Oedipus Rex*, one of his most influential plays.

licly. Perhaps he felt he had a dignified reputation to protect at court. He would not embarrass the king. And *Bacon* had powerful enemies who would have tried to make any role he may have taken in the production of those plays to be treasonous, or at least scandalous.

Bacon was, nevertheless, eventually trapped in scandal. After his disgrace at court on trumped-up charges, the royalists resisted any deeper investigation of the source of the Shakespearean plays. *Bacon* could never be accepted as possibly the most important playwright in British history; that would be too much of a slap to the British sense of propriety. Thus, the *Bacon*/Shakespeare connection was buried.

That brings us to the formation of the Theosophical Society. This arhat—the former Pythagorean elder, *Sophocles, R. Bacon, F. Bacon*—had, in the early eighteenth century, yet another life, in Kashmir. In that life, he was the son of a wealthy aristocratic family of the Hindu/Moslem Sikh tradition. *Kuthumi Lal Singh* was his name. Through spiritual discipline and training, through surrender to God and an uncompromising commitment to higher truth in that life, he entered the higher spheres of knowledge and enlightenment. He took the last step for a human being, that of spiritual ascension.

Although this former arhat has permanently entered the final soul realm as a fifth-degree initiate, he has chosen to remain in contact with earth as an elder and teacher. This is the *Master Kuthumi (K. H.)* of Helena Blavatsky and of the Theosophical Society.

Helena Blavatsky
Burned at the Stake

Helena Blavatsky published *Isis Unveiled* in 1877 and *The Secret Doctrine* in 1888, as well as several other major works on assorted subjects of esoteric teaching—both oriental and occidental. Controversy swirled around her: strange stories, secret powers, seances, mysterious masters of wisdom. Who was this woman?

For students unfamiliar with, or frankly unfriendly toward, theosophy, *When Daylight Comes*, by Howard Murphet is recommended reading.

Helena Petrovna Blavatsky
(Aug. 12, 1831—May 8, 1891)

Helena Blavatsky, who co-founded the Theosophical Society in New York in 1875, was a reincarnation of the Italian Renaissance philosopher *Giordano Bruno*. Some theosophists believed that *Blavatsky's* disciple Annie Besant had been *Giordano Bruno*. This error is understandable; *Blavatsky's* aura and mental energy dominated Besant. (It is even more complicated than that, as we will see in the Besant study that follows.)

Helena Blavatsky was the daughter of a Russian aristocratic family. Her natural psychic ability, indomitable will and intellectual curiosity led her to become one of modern times' most courageous pioneers in the realm of occult investigation and synthesis of universal esoteric principles.

Helena Blavatsky was a "thought-warrior," a genius on a spiritual mission, who was supported by elder teachers of the inner school of wisdom. Our research indicates that behind the formation of the Theosophical Society was a true spiritual master, among the greatest humanity has yet produced. Make no mistake about it, *Blavatsky* was truly guided and protected by her beloved master, and her direction was with the light of God. Her work had a creative dimension to it that was guided by her spirit. As much as some may not care for this conclusion, Christendom owes *Helena Blavatsky* a debt of gratitude.

She dedicated her life to the creation of a society that could introduce, by intellectual and spiritual means, compelling new thoughts into public theological debate. It was these ideas, extracted from old traditions and brought into the public mind through the work of the Theosophical Society, that paved the way for our generation's openness to the world's philosophies—be they Moslem, Buddhist, Hindu or Christian.

Blavatsky's enemy[36] was the demon of inquisition. Inquisition is a powerful thought monster that lurks in the shadows of the collectives of all our root-cultures—especially the Judeo-Christian and Moslem traditions. Who but one who had died at the hands of the Inquisition would be better qualified to carry the message of universal esoteric openness?

As a cultural universalist, *Blavatsky* was one of the great religious philosophers and humanitarian social leaders of the nineteenth century. She exposed the Christian community to points of truth and spiritual reality that needed to be integrated into understanding. The motto of the Theosophical Society is: "There is no religion higher than truth."

Blavatsky was vilified, out of jealousy and fear, by those who felt that her truth would somehow harm their own. She seemed to invite controversy. She did not pay careful attention to the ap-

---

[36] This will be better understood when we look at a former life of Henry Steel Olcott, co-founder and first president of the Theosophical Society.

pearances of her personal behavior. Although she fought back against vicious press attacks, since she had not used great discrimination in her personal choices, the scandal mongers had a field day.

At the very least, women worldwide owe the indomitable *Helena Blavatsky* a debt as one of the world's first, and most courageous, international feminists. It is easy, for those who so choose, to love to dislike her; however, that view should be reconsidered. The following quotes from *Blavatsky's Isis Unveiled* capture the essence of her lifelong struggle for philosophical freedom against any intellectual tyranny imposed by a political system engaged in theological or philosophical sophistry or socioreligious bigotry:

> *Christianity is on trial, and has been, ever since science felt strong enough to act as Public Prosecutor. A portion of the case we are drafting in this book. What of truth is there in this Theology? Through what sects has it been transmitted? Whence was it primarily derived? To answer, we must trace the history of the World Religion, alike through the secret Christian sects as through those of other great religious subdivisions of the race; for the Secret Doctrine is the Truth, and that religion is nearest divine that has contained it with least adulteration.*

H.P.B. Isis Unveiled, Vol. 2, Ch. VII

167

> *Deeply sensible of the Titanic struggle that is now in progress between materialism and the spiritual aspirations of mankind, our constant endeavor has been to gather into our several chapters, like weapons into armories, every fact and argument that can be used to aid the latter in defeating the former. Sickly and deformed child as it now is, the materialism of today is born of the brutal yesterday. Unless its growth is arrested, it may become our master. It is the bastard progeny of the French Revolution and its reaction against ages of religious bigotry and repression. To prevent the crushing of these spiritual aspirations, the blighting of these hopes, and the deadening of that intuition which teaches us of a God and a hereafter, we must show*

our false theologies in their naked deformity, and distinguish between divine religion and human dogmas. Our voice is raised for spiritual freedom, and our plea made for enfranchisement from all tyranny, whether of Science or Theology.

H.P.B. Isis Unveiled, Vol 1, Preface, final paragraph.

Giordano Bruno
(1548—Feb. 17, 1600)

168

Giordano Bruno is one of the best-known philosophers of sixteenth century Europe. A Dominican priest[37] and Italian Renaissance genius, *Bruno* was accused of heresy for the unrestrained reach of his thought. In 1576, he was driven out of his order. He found temporary refuge in Protestant England.

Giordano Bruno taught at Oxford in 1583. Francis Bacon had entered Cambridge at the age of twelve, ten years earlier. In 1583, Francis Bacon was at the height of his intellectual development. These two did, in fact, have direct contact, resulting in mutual admiration. Francis Bacon—the former Franciscan Roger Bacon and former Pythagorean elder—was unconsciously irresistible to *Bruno*. At the same time, because *Bruno* was older and a renowned Italian teacher, he assumed the role of mentor for Bacon. Although not himself a former Pythagorean, *Bruno* had studied and ad-

---

[37] The Dominicans are a Catholic order that has a past-life connection to an honorable Persian/Zoroastrian priestcraft.

mired the Pythagoreans in more than one life. In meeting the youthful Bacon, *Bruno* met in physical incarnation the soul of a former Pythagorean elder.

After teaching for a time at Oxford, *Bruno* returned to the Continent. He did not, however, stay out of trouble with the Inquisition. He was imprisoned, in 1592, for his teachings and writings. When pressured by the authorities, he refused to recant. *Giordano Bruno* was burned at the stake on February 17, 1600. In allowing this great offense, the Catholic Church set fire to the wall of its own religious pretensions, releasing an incendiary energy that would return to haunt it.

Based on this insight, it is fascinating to read in *Helena Blavatsky's* biography that, at her baptism as an infant in Russia, she screamed uncontrollably and kicked over a candle that set fire to the robe of the officiating priest. *Helena's* mother and aunts saw this as auspicious.

Henry Steel Olcott
The Christian Root of Theosophy

Col. Henry Steel Olcott
(1832—Feb. 7, 1907)

In this study, we see an amazing tie between early Christian gnosticism and the formation of the theosophical movement. The first international president of the Theosophical Society, *Henry Steel Olcott*, was a veteran of the American Civil War as a supply colonel for the Union army. After the war, he became a journalist, writing for the New York newspaper the *Daily Graphic*.

In 1874, *Olcott* was on assignment investigating psychic phenomenon in Vermont. His articles on spiritualistic manifestations came to the attention of Helena Blavatsky, who was then in New York City. She immediately traveled to the Vermont "ghost house," as it was called.

Blavatsky had a premonition that *Olcott* would become her partner in the formation of a worldwide organization dedicated to the study of spiritual phenomena. *Olcott* and Blavatsky hit it off right away. As a moral preacher and practical propagandist/ organizer, *Olcott* provided a conservative balance for Blavatsky's irrepressible, fearless and often disorganized enthusiasm.

Olcott was a champion of universal truth and ecumenical brotherhood in world religion. After his conversion to Buddhism, which may have been due in part to his rejection of the false sense of superiority and closed-mindedness of nineteenth century Christian culture, he became a champion of equal educational opportunity for Buddhist youth. *Olcott* founded numerous Buddhist schools for children in several countries under British colonial occupation. Some British colonial authorities mistrusted and even disliked *Olcott*, attempting to drive him out of more than one country. Once again, this reflects the British/Egyptian karmic connection since *Origen* had been driven out of Egypt.

Olcott and Blavatsky's association was certainly not accidental. Unknown to *Olcott* at that time, he was preparing for a spiritual mission. This preparedness is obvious from the perspective of the Akashic Records. This soul lived as one of early Christianity's most famous Gnostic fathers, preachers and writers. He was the Christian father *Origen*, who believed in reincarnation and was one of Christianity's earliest champions of universal philosophy and benevolence to diverse religions.

Origen
(c. 185—c. 254)

Olcott's joining of a Buddhist order reflected his deep need to embrace both mysticism and the benevolent teaching of nonviolence, a Christian principle that has often been ignored by Christian sects. Could he come to terms with violence; could he even forgive it? This is a difficult question for a former army colonel. Could he raise his spiritual consciousness to the righteousness of acceptance? Could he forgive the problem of false spiritual authority that he had experienced from the Christian leadership of Alexandria, in the life as *Origen*? Could he avoid becoming a false authority in his own way, in his life as *Olcott*? These karmic questions, and more, apply here.

Superficially, the personalities of *Olcott* and *Origen* may seem distant. However, circumstances of personality and cultural expectation, as well as educational opportunity, must be taken into account. If you follow-up on a study of the biographies of both *Origen* and *Olcott*, you will see how well these two lives fit together.

Origen was born to Christian parents near Alexandria, Egypt. He received an education under the Christian theologian, Clement of Alexandria, who introduced him to Neoplatonism, a direction that ultimately led to theosophy. He also studied with Ammonius. *Origen's* father was killed by the mobs in the persecutions of 202, and *Origen* barely escaped that fate himself. At an early age, after Clement's death, *Origen* became the principal of the Christian Catechetical School of Alexandria.

Due as much to his moral character as to his writing, *Origen* attracted large numbers of students and interested people to his teaching. Although not yet a full priest, he traveled widely to Caesarea and Jerusalem, where he preached sermons. The Bishop of Alexandria did not like his violation of custom—that of preaching without permission—and demanded he stop. When *Origen* returned to Alexandria, the Bishop of Alexandria excommunicated him.

Returning to the Holy Land, *Origen* established a school of theology in Caesarea in 231, which he headed for 20 years. Perhaps most important to our study is the focus of *Origen's* theological teaching, which attempted to synthesize Christian scripture and belief with Greek philosophy, specifically Neoplatonism.

Origen taught that the highest good is to become as much like God as possible through progressive illumination (*theosis*). Not to distract from the Christian orientation of *Origen's* beliefs, this also resembles Buddhist mysticism. That *Origen* forsook his conservative Christian cultural roots, in another life, to embrace theosophy and eventually profess a catechism of Buddhism, is no surprise. His teaching, in a strange karmic way, may have been largely responsible for the incorporation of universal and Gnostic premises in Catholic theology.

Origen's belief in reincarnation was not accepted by later Catholic theologians. As they rose in influence, their disbelief led to the exorcism of *Origin's* teaching from Catholicism. The Origenistic school was declared heretical and officially excluded from Catholic theology in 553. *Origen*, however, continued to play an important undercover role in Catholicism.

Origen's life ended painfully; he suffered a slow death from the torture he received when the Christian persecutions resumed in 250. *Olcott's* severe headaches, which he suffered until they were removed by his master, were a karmic remnant of this time of separation from his priestly roots, as well as a remembrance of pain suffered at the hands of cruel tormentors. *Olcott* may or may not have been permanently healed of these headaches; in any case, they were set aside during that life's service for the good of the work.

173

Annie Besant
Human Progress of an Angel

This soul was an angel who had never before incarnated into human life. His/her first life on earth was as *Jeanne d'Arc*, the enigmatic and charismatic girl-soldier of France, the *Maid of Orleans*. The *Jeanne d'Arc* story has inspired millions. It is one of the all-time great spiritual passion plays on the world stage of life.

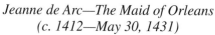

Jeanne de Arc—The Maid of Orleans
(c. 1412—May 30, 1431)

174

   At the age of fifteen, a French peasant girl began to hear voices. She saw visions that told her she should go to the dauphin, the future Charles VII, and inform him that he should be crowned king of France. She was afraid at first, but her voices continued to urge her to be brave, to be a warrior of spirit. "Go to the dauphin," they said. "Have courage, have faith, obey."

   Who knows if true inner guidance would compel a girl to put on armor and pick up a sword? War is brutal. But, in any case, this energetic young warrior of spirit, who was all of nineteen years old, followed her voices and went to the dauphin. She was able to convince herself, and him, that she could lead the French army to victory against the British in the Hundred Years War.

   The life of *Jeanne d' Arc* exemplifies the type of spiritual struggle present in a soul that has come, at long last, to the first degree of initiation. Courage of conviction, commitment to truth, a stand against evil, faith in God, tested by the dark force of resistance—all of these are present in the *Jeanne d'Arc* passion play.

In a normal human evolutionary process, it takes many hundreds, even thousands, of lives to achieve spiritual nobility, courage and obedience to a higher spiritual calling. This angel started her first encounter on earth with the "anointing of God," the sign of a first-degree initiate—and it took place within just one lifetime. This is a messiah story. The true initiates, as a principle, are chosen and anointed of God; thus, they are messiahs in truth. *Jeanne d'Arc* was such a soul, having suffered the first great anointing.

The basics of *Jeanne's* story are true, although it has entered the history books fictionalized as inspiration. *Jeanne* was, in her higher nature, angelic in origin. She experienced inner spiritual epiphany; she truly had visions and heard voices. Interpreting this guidance correctly was her test. Who, after all, in Catholic France of that century knew how such voices should be approached? Who knew what they were, or what they might mean? The future king believed; or did he?

Charles VII used *Jeanne d'Arc's* public inspiration willingly and to his advantage. It is probable that it was his idea to dress her in armor and a sword. After the dauphin's coronation as the king of France, *Jeanne* disobeyed him by following her voices. She regrouped "her" army to go to the relief of Compiegne, without the support of the king. Was she guided or was she *willfully* unwilling to accept practical obedience from a mere mortal king? The battle of Compiegne was *Jeanne 's* undoing, her "one battle too far," so to speak. Unrestrained enthusiasm seems to have brought her downfall. She was captured and turned over to the Inquisition.

Perhaps this was indeed all a predetermined French collective passion play, of which *Jeanne* was the designated star. Or, perhaps, this was the necessary alchemical fire that would temper the anointing of her spiritual light; again, who knows? In the course of her story, disobedience toward her king and a head-strong personal willfulness led her into defeat. When *Jeanne d'Arc* was captured by the British, Charles VII did not attempt to rescue her—or, again, so it seems.

What was this all about? What was this young angel learning? Her time in prison is a moving story of political intrigue and psychic oppression. She was turned over to the Inquisition because the British civil authorities were afraid of her potential influence as a martyr. Over the course of time, under psychological torture, she was tricked into recanting; perhaps her voices were not from God. Later, *Jeanne* retracted her recantation, accusing the priests of tricking her, saying that her voices were indeed from God and not from the devil. She stood alone, facing death.

Her retraction gave the Inquisition prosecutors their chance. She could now be condemned, with destruction by fire. And she was. Accused of witchcraft and of being a relapsed heretic, *Jeanne de Arc* was burned at the stake on May 30, 1431. One wonders what influence her story had on Giordano Bruno a hundred years later, when it was his turn to burn at the stake. Bruno would not compromise his beliefs and recant.

Jeanne de Arc's momentary confusion and recantation affected the life and personality of her soul's next life, in which any compromise with truth was unthinkable. We find in this next life the higher development of the angel's great mental capacity through a gentle, reclusive but brilliant personality.

This angel—who as *Jeanne de Arc* was tortured by the hand of man, yet was loved by God—reincarnated fairly quickly into another life in seventeenth century Europe. No longer Catholic, having been excommunicated by flame, he was born into a Portuguese-Jewish family, who had fled Spanish persecution to the safe haven of Holland. This male child (his true polarity) became the famous philosopher and metaphysician *Benedict de Spinoza*.

Spinoza drew spiritual and intellectual inspiration from the life and writings of the philosopher heretic and martyr Giordano Bruno, forming a connection that would endure across the centuries. Accused of religious heresy and free-thinking, *Spinoza* was eventually expelled from his synagogue and exiled from the Jewish community of Amsterdam. In spring 1673, living in poverty, he was offered the Chair of Philosophy at Heidelberg. He declined in order to protect his personal freedom of expression. Perhaps he wished to avoid any professional obligation to defend his work.

Spinoza's influence was enormous. This humble lens grinder from Amsterdam, who expressed in his work the fulfillment of a second-degree initiate, was one of the clearest thinkers of all time. Due to his influence on many other thinkers, he has been called the "founder of modern philosophy."

A study of *Spinoza's* works is valuable to the student of Akashic history. The very idea that an angel was struggling with these human concerns and abstract intellectual concepts is, in itself, both interesting and inspiring. His next life unfolds as that of the famous social activist and theosophist, *Annie Besant* of England.

Benedict de Spinoza
(Nov. 24, 1632— Feb. 21, 1677)
Annie Besant
(Oct. 1, 1847—Sept. 30, 1933)

Annie Besant was the second international president of the Theosophical Society. She was a social activist from a very early age. Married at twenty to an Anglican clergyman, she separated from him five years later and declared herself independent. She had a full life ahead of her. In nineteenth century England *Besant* (the "firebrand") found no shortage of social, political and intellectual causes.

By the 1880s, she had became a well-known Socialist activist; she was even called an atheist by her detractors. In the social pressure cooker of Victorian England, she developed into an exceptionally fine writer and public speaker. Her reputation was well-established in the public arena long before she met Helena Blavatsky and joined the Theosophical Society in 1889.

Upon meeting Blavatsky, *Besant's* conversion to theosophy was immediate.[38] Their spiritual recognition was direct and mutual. These two were part of a greater spiritual plan, organized at a divine level, with a conscious mission awareness. The one whom *Spinoza* had admired the most in all the world was Bruno. It was a karmic magnetism.

Karmically influenced by the life of *Jeanne d'Arc*, *Besant* also carried the spiritual sword, or mission, of emancipation. She became a warrior for truth and freedom, fighting against male domination; cultural, religious and intellectual oppression; and spiritual ignorance—in every form she encountered them. To *Besant*, Blavatsky was the "general" for whom she had waited. She joined this woman's "army" and, to the wonder of millions, became a soldier for the cause.

After her conversion to theosophy in 1889, *Annie Besant* left England for India. From that time on, India became her permanent home. She founded the Central Hindu College at Varanasi. She was also, for many years, Indo-European editor for several publications and periodicals, publishing many books of her own.[39] She traveled the world on lecture tours, always returning to her homebase in India. She eventually became an important intellectual supporter of India's home-rule independence movement against British colonial occupation. Once again, we see the spirit of *Jeanne d'Arc* moving against the British, to aid a country in throwing off British occupation and establishing self-rule.

178

As a point of interest, *Annie Besant* had a lifelong friendship with the British playwright George Bernard Shaw. It is an interesting karmic syncronicity that Shaw later wrote the famous play *Saint Joan*. This play was, in part, Shaw's response to the Catholic canonization of *Jeanne d'Arc* in 1920. In later years, Shaw made some critical remarks about *Besant*. He became resentful,

---

[38] Keep in mind: the former *Benedict de Spinoza* was meeting the former Giordano Bruno.

[39] Recommended reading is *A Study in Consciousness,* by *Annie Besant,* published in India in 1904.

it seems, when his former colleague went off to India to follow that "strange" Helena Blavatsky. Shaw may have been the type of patriarchal male who, although professing to be liberal, could not really accept that a women could be so intelligent or so independent. At least he felt a need to depreciate her for it.

In his play *Saint Joan,* Bernard Shaw had *Joan* pray, "O God that madest this beautiful earth, when will it be ready to receive Thy saints?" Well, in the case of *Annie Besant,* India did "call" to and "receive" her. Her work inspired thousands, including Mahatma Gandhi. *Besant* went to the poor and suffering in Mother India to uplift their condition; she was not, however, willing to settle for any role less than advisor to the king. An hierarchical, even elitist, assumption was apparently at work in *Besant's* expectations. Perhaps this is what an angel would expect. It was a role that India accepts of its saints. In suffering personal difficulties, this lofty soul earned her ruffled angel wings. We are reminded of the saying that "only fools rush in where angels fear to tread." While coming to earth can prove to be a great difficulty, in her higher Self, *Besant* followed the path of the Living Christ, as all angels must.[40]

Socially, emotionally, intellectually and spiritually—in terms of collective influence—*Annie Besant* left a greater legacy to the world through her work with the Theosophical Society than had either of her two previous lives. She suffered the trials and met the challenges to her beliefs in a manner equal to that of a third-degree initiate. She achieved the permanent Godly detachment of a spiritually enlightened saint. Her true degree of initiation occurred in her higher Selfhood upon completion of that life, when the angel and her humanity merged.

In the mortal life of *Annie Besant*, we see the suffering of personal loneliness and even a few years of diminished mental capacity at the end of her life. Such personal difficulty occasionally

---

[40] This is not to assume that her causes and choices were enlightened. All souls entering earth life must learn to choose right understanding and right action, and sometimes this is preceded by error and suffering. Until spiritual mastery, this is true for all souls, including initiates.

surrounds an initiate who is completing the path of return—the third degree of initiation. *Besant* was a beautiful, wise and strong soul, one who's life had a lasting effect on collective growth. Her life remains one of the great spiritual lights of the twentieth century. Some of her personal choices may have been less than perfect, but through her innermost being she offered a gift of love as a spiritual warrior in service to God. For an angel to enter the human social milieu is a great act of courage and sacrifice. Can we be anything but grateful? Such a series of lives as these can only be judged by the remnant gifts that they have left for humanity.

Aquinas-Kant
From Theology to Reason

We now turn to two great philosopher souls who have spent many lifetimes on earth developing their mental abilities—from China to France, Greece, England and Germany. For such thinkers as these, theology, philosophy and reason are of greater interest than anything else in God's reality. It is beyond the scope of this work, however, to discuss their thoughts in detail. You can conduct this intellectual analysis independently if you are interested.

Intellectuals seldom, if ever, recognize their own limits. They may discuss the problem of limits, but they continue as if their thought were the ground of reality. The question is one of circles within circles of the mind. There are two primary spiritual paths of the return: the path of the heart (e.g., the arts, mysticism, devotion) and the path of the mind (e.g., philosophy, theology, science, occultism). Among mystics of the Christian Church and mystics of other communities of faith, it is understood that, while both paths are legitimate, only one doorway exists—that of the heart.

Heart-centered mystics may accept the mental exercises of theology as valuable, even of great service to a lost or wandering humanity. Ultimately, however, such exercises do not carry intrinsic spiritual authority, except perhaps to inspire understanding that leads to an awareness of self-deception. Metaphorically speaking, it has been said that the anti-Christ is confronted in intellect; thus, the "devil incarnate" can influence the understanding of any religious group through intellectualized authority.

We, as souls on the great path of spiritual evolution and return to God, do not need intellectualized theology. What we do need is to not become deluded in theology, or to become arrogant, or to dominate others due to some imagined intellectual superiority formed in a religious context. There is nothing inherent in intellect to be proud of, or to justify spiritual elitism or pride. Jesus, upon whom Christianity was founded, although mentally powerful, nevertheless expressed himself primarily through heart energy, never writing a word. Jesus even made a point, reported in scripture, that the disciples were not to make their worship like the scribes, or Pharisees. His disciples were not to be seen before others to be higher or more spiritual in any way. This, from the Gospels, is worth recalling as we review past lives and the teachings of former Church theologians and compare their thoughts with those of other philosophers.

The work of such clear thinkers as Benedict de Spinoza, who was accused of being a mere rationalist, a modernistic pantheist, set the tone for the movement of modern rationality, away from its roots in medieval theology. Many pure empiricists and sense rationalists joined the fray, engaging in intellectual competition and presenting their thought as the truest approach to reality. No disrespect is intended; this is not meant as cynicism. We need good teachers in the realm of ideas; their work is like a hot air balloon that helps lift the collective thought of humanity out of its archaic mire of superstition and speculative foolishness. It is beneficial for us, as students of the inner life, to review the highest thoughts of such teachers. In comparing ideas of various thinkers, we can nurture the God-given powers of our own minds. Then, with humility regarding all human intellectual constructs, and with maturity of mind, we can grow spiritually.

Thomas Aquinas
(1224—March 7, 1274)

Thomas Aquinas is one of the most loved and respected theologians of the modern Catholic Church. The importance of his influence cannot be overestimated. His thought formed a bridge from ancient to modern times and successfully claimed legitimacy in the form of Christian dogma. If anyone could accomplish such a task of synthesis, it was *Aquinas.*

Thomas Aquinas spent his life building an intellectual haven for Christian philosophy. However, shortly before his death, after having quit writing his last great thesis after an experience of spiritual epiphany, he reportedly said, "Knowing what I now know, I would not have written a word."

When *Aquinas* was a boy, perhaps five years old, his little sister was killed by lightening while walking with him on a road near his home, by a monastery. The boy was later told by his ambitious and aristocratic mother that he was intended for God. She wished him to become the abbot of the local monastery. This was intended to consolidate the family's aristocratic influence. However, it had a more profound, personal effect on this young, temperamental and sensitive genius. God, he came to believe, was a frightening power that must be reckoned with, for he could give or take away at will.

And so *Aquinas* was sent off to the monks to be educated. Trauma at an early age tends to become a permanent part of one's unconscious psyche and *Aquinas* never fully recovered from the frightening death of his little sister. Out of that trauma came a life of emotional theology, and a need to understand and apologize for God. This attempt to find salvation and protection from destruction can be traced in the unspoken message of his work which, despite its grand intellectual style, carries an element of separation between mind and emotion.

In *Aquinas'* epiphany, at the end of his life, he may have reached wholeness, moving beyond thinking and losing all desire to reason with theological constructs. As an intellectual genius, he would not stop thinking. He might, however, take an entirely different approach in his next life in an attempt to conquer all pretension of mentality by placing a final limit on reason. We find this great thinker returning to a life in Germany with an even stronger sword and shield, and a sharper scalpel, intended to tame the beast of intellectuality.

Thomas Aquinas reincarnated as the German philosopher *Immanuel Kant.*

Immanuel Kant
(Apr. 22, 1724—Feb. 12, 1804)

This soul has labored to become one of the great thinkers of all time. His focus on the process of mental ideation is so strong that it seems at times he is barely anchored in his earth life. He is a champion for the light; there is no doubt about that.

Thomas Aquinas met a challenge posed to Christian faith by the philosophical achievements of the Greeks and Arabs and, thus, developed a synthesis of faith and reason. *Immanuel Kant*, in his turn, altered the nature of philosophical inquiry. Some have referred to *Kant's* work as a "Copernican revolution" in philosophy. *Kant* met a powerful challenge to the spiritual gates of the mind and higher intuition by negating the scientific schools of empiricism. The empiricist position, presented in cynical perfection by Sir David Hume, (whose study follows) held that the mind can only know that which is presented by the senses. This philosophy limited human psychic potential to an earth-bound model.

Kant entered life with a spiritual mission to close the door to past errors of intellectual hubris and to open a door to the possible by defining absolute limits to the scope of reason. He brought with him from his soul life a finely honed mental scalpel to cut to the core of what can be known, and how it is known, by reason. *Kant* left open doors beyond reason—to faith, to a higher reality, to avenues of direct knowledge of God. Knowledge of God cannot be proven or even legitimately argued by reason alone, nor can reason claim superiority in the field of inner knowledge.

This represents a small fragment of *Kant's* work. With regard to the karmic track of continuance between *Aquinas* and *Kant*, we can identify a serious mental and emotional detachment in both lives, but in opposite directions. *Aquinas* worked from deeply shattered emotional feelings; his life was overshadowed by a need for emotional reconstruction. *Kant*, equally unwhole, kept his feelings out of his mental exercises. A root to these lives can be traced to early China and the beginning of the Taoist tradition. We can track *Aquinas* to an earlier life as the less famous disciple, *Guo Xiang*, of the Taoist master Zuangzi (or Chuang Tsu).

Guo Xiang
(399—295 B.C.)

Chuang Tsu (or Zuangzi), one of the foremost of the Chinese Taoist mystics, had a disciple *Guo Xiang*, who was less well-known than his mentor. You are asked to follow intuitively this connection that stretches from the Roman Neoplatonist philosopher Plotinus and Iamblichus to *Thomas Aquinas's* teacher Albertus Magnus. *Aquinas* was influenced by the teachings of each of these persons, all of whose lives connect back to Chuang Tsu, whose influence is pivotal in this study. (More will be presented in the Albertus Magnus study.)

Souls whose primary focus is mental and intellectual tend to mix their inner signatures so completely with their favored and loved teachers that they take on the same karmic energy. As a result, it is sometimes difficult to discriminate between their higher mental energies. Plotinus, Iamblichus, Albertus Magnus and *Thomas Aquinas* all originated from a similar line of discipleship in the early Chinese philosophical tradition. A strong karmic loop exists between China (with its Taoist, Confucian, Buddhist mix) and France (with its Christian scholasticism) as well as with other early centers of European philosophy and theology.

As in the case of early Protestantism, both Holland (with Spinoza) and Germany (with *Kant*) participated in a revolution of religious thought. Such reformation movements are necessary. They have led archaic European Christian theology, ever so slowly, back to a renewal of temporal enlightenment. Perhaps Taoism, Confucianism and even archaic Buddhism were also brought quietly toward a more rational enlightenment through the work of these leaders, who in spirit are still loved and unconsciously sought after by the Chinese collective. The evolution of human consciousness is progressing slowly forward as our understanding of the light and the limits of reason is purified, leading us higher, beyond temporal understanding to the reality of a true spiritual illumination.

Ockham and Hume
Another Heretic

William of Ockham, or *Occum*, was one of the most influential philosopher-theologians of his time. Born in England in 1285, a few years after the death of Thomas Aquinas, he studied at Oxford and entered the Franciscan order. As a result of *Ockham's* study and advocacy of the Greek philosopher Aristotle, he was accused of heresy. He was called to trial in France, where he unsuccessfully attempted to defend his position. Together with the minister-general of the Franciscans, he fled the papal court at Avignon. They were excommunicated, but received protection from Holy Roman Emperor Louis IV, an enemy of the Pope at that time.

It was in the emperor's court that *Ockham* did the majority of his writing, rejecting several of the premises of Thomas Aquinas. We sense an adverse karmic energy between the mind set of Aquinas and that of *Ockham*. *Ockham* reincarnated in Scotland in 1711 as *David Hume*.

William of Ockham
(1285—1349)

Sir David Hume
(May 7, 1711—Aug. 25, 1776)

Sir David Hume entered the University of Edinburgh at the age of 12, where he studied law. After completing his university degree, he decided to pursue a life of study. He moved to France, where he wrote his famous *Treatise on Human Nature* at the age of 29.

It is interesting to note that *Hume* is credited with believing in reincarnation. At what point in his life he expressed this is unknown but, if true, may indicate an intuitive breakthrough for this philosopher.

Both *Hume* and Kant became leaders of entire schools of thought; however, of the two, Kant was the true spiritual initiate of an early degree, although which degree is not easy to discern. *Hume*, while brilliant, was not yet a spiritual initiate. As we have noted before, a demonstration of high intellectual capacity is not necessarily a measure of spiritual enlightenment. A further comparison of these lives would be of value.

Jan Hus
Disciple of Jesus

*Andrew, Disciple of Jesus
(d. 60 A.D.)*

Former disciples of Jesus, known and unknown, represent the karmic progress of the historical mission of the Church, but not necessarily in its present-day form. The written record of the names of the twelve male disciples of Jesus is somewhat inexact. One, whom we will now study, was among the twelve original male disciples. Several women were among the inner circle of disciples, but not within the group of twelve. We have been able to identify only three of the twelve who have reincarnated into other famous lives in the West. (Other studies will follow.) These three—*Andrew*, Peter and Bartholomew—have since reincarnated into active evangelism in the ongoing karmic flow of what may be called the "historic ideation of the Church." At some point in their future lives, these three became independent-minded enough to create personal karma in their religious choices.

   Other lives connected with the soul of the disciple *Andrew* are *Athanasius*, in the fourth century; the Morovian Catholic/Protestant reformer *Jan Hus*; in the fourteenth century, *John Wesley* of the Church of England, founder of Methodism, in the eighteenth century; and in the twentieth century the Chinese Protestant evangelist *Watchman Nee*. These connections demonstrate an amazing span of cultural communities.

Athanasius, secretary to the Bishop of Alexandria in the fourth century, having received a classical education, was sent as a theological expert from Alexandria to the First Council of Nicaea in 325. Among his early writings was *On the Incarnation of the Word,* that brought the orthodox doctrine of Redemption, which he argued at the Council of Nicaea, to its fullest expression. The Catholic Athanasian Creed is named after him, but was not of his making. This life is interesting both for its strengths and its weaknesses, and should be studied carefully for a full grasp of early Catholic ideas.

Athanasius, Bishop of Alexandria　　　　*Jan Hus*
(c. 295—373)　　　　　*(c. 1372—July 6, 1415)*

The Czech religious reformer *Jan Hus* was perhaps one of the most influential early Protestants in Europe. His life is one of the great tragic stories in the history of the organized Church; with insights drawn from an understanding of his past lives, his story is even more significant.

Jan Hus defended the writing of the early English Protestant theologian John Wycliffe. Like Wycliffe, *Hus* published scathing condemnations of political corruption within the Church. In 1409, partially due to popular support, *Hus* was appointed rector of the University of Prague. Forced to choose sides between two rival claimants to the papal throne, he was forbidden to preach in 1409, and was excommunicated in

1411. In defiance of papal orders, he published *De Ecclesia* in 1413.

Another Church council was called in 1414 (the Council of Constance) with the intention of healing the great schism of the papacy. *Hus* was promised safe conduct by Holy Roman Emperor Sigismund. Within a month, however, he was arrested, condemned for heresy and burned at the stake. Thus, he became a martyr and his proposed reforms became the rallying point for Czech independence. His followers, the Hussites, were early exponents of Protestant Reformation. They later formed the Morovian Church.

In its next life, this soul was born in England as *John Wesley*, who became famous as a Protestant reformer. A note of karmic correspondence can easily be perceived between the early life and education of *John Wesley*, father of Methodism, and *Jan Hus*. *Wesley's* mother was the driving force in his moral and academic education. The story of his mother's rescue of her young son John (whom she called "Jackie") from a burning building has become legendary in Methodist history.[41]

John Wesley   Watchman Nee
(June 28, 1703— Mar. 2, 1791)   *(c. 1903—May 30, 1972)*

Born into a well-to-do family, *Wesley* attended Charterhouse School and then Oxford, where he studied at Christ Church. In 1726, he was elected a fellow of Lincoln College and, in 1728, he

---

[41] Think about that; consider the emotional appeal of *Jan Hus* martyrdom at the stake.

was ordained in the Church of England. *Wesley's* conversion to evangelism was directly connected to a group that was an outgrowth of the scattered Czech Morovian (Hussite) movement, then flourishing underground in England. This interesting chapter in the history of Christian reformation is one of "born again" evangelism, persecutions, escape to the Americas and later a return to a more receptive British social environment. *Wesley's* life stands as one of the great beacons of light for the progress of the organized Christian Church toward enlightenment. This type of leadership is characteristic of a first-degree initiate.

John Wesley envisioned worldwide Christian evangelism. In his next life, this soul was again called by that vision into a new area of social reform—as the Chinese evangelist, poet, propagandist and political prisoner, *Watchman Nee.*

Watchman Nee began his ministry in China in 1923. A virtual unknown outside China during his lifetime, he has become world-famous. The inspiration of his life and pen has touched millions of souls; *Nee's* life story is especially inspiring to Chinese Christians because of his insistence on a Chinese-based Protestant theology.

Nee died in Kwan Chao, China in 1972, at the age of sixty-nine, shortly after his release from prison. In 1952, he had been given a fifteen-year prison sentence, convicted by Communist authorities on charges of being a counter-revolutionary influence. *Nee* served a full twenty years as a political prisoner in mainland China, having been given an extra five years for being unrepentant.

Watchman Nee's biography, entitled *Against the Tide,* was written by Angus Kinnear, a British Christian missionary to India, and was published in 1973 in England. *Nee's* own writing first became known outside China with the publication of his *The Normal Christian Life,* which appeared in print in India in 1957. Since this was five years into *Nee's* imprisonment, it is unlikely that he ever knew that his life and work were appreciated in the West. Other writings by *Watchmen Nee,* that eventually found their way to the West include *Love Not the World; What Shall This Man Do?; A Table in the Wilderness; Sit, Walk, Stand; Study Guide to The Normal Christian Life; Changed into His Likeness; The Joyful Heart.*

Martin Luther
Protestant "Disciple"

The past-life history of *Martin Luther*, famed German Protestant reformer, is most interesting. He is featured dramatically and karmically in stories in both the Old and New Testaments. He is also one of two souls who have been Pope *twice*.[42]

As previously discussed, once a soul has been mentioned in the Bible, or in any sacred literature, and is loved by millions, its karmic course tends to become magnetically entrained to that particular collective expectation. This is especially true if the soul concerned is not a spiritual initiate, or does not possess a higher mandate of spiritual destiny. In the case of non-initiates, many may have power in a human sense but not yet choice in a spiritual sense. Thus, they become firmly locked to the wheel of karma.

Martin Luther has, by now, become a first-degree initiate, bordering on the second degree of initiation. He is also on the path of the first ray—the ray of government and leadership. Notice that socio-religious leadership is the strongest and most consistent theme that ties this soul's lives together.[43] We begin *Martin Luther's* study with the life of *Nehemiah* of the Old Testament, as told in the *Book of Nehemiah*.

Nehemiah was a Hebrew councilor to the Persian king. He was a wise and respected councilor, one who gained great wealth and influence. In a time of personal religious crisis, *Nehemiah* requested of the king that he be permitted to return to the ruined city of Jerusalem to lead

---

[42] The second soul is Pope John Paul II, who was formerly Pope Innocent I.
[43] The first ray, that of leadership, is one of the slowest paths in human evolution. The focus of such as these tends to be more often on the earth plane, especially on affairs of social order, or business. It is their strength in earthly matters, and their practical focus, that slows down their spiritual development.

the Babylonian Jews who wanted to return to their Holy City.[44]

Nehemiah
(c. 350 B.C.)

Nicodemus
(c. 35 B.C.)

We find *Nehemiah* reincarnated in Jerusalem as a wealthy Jew and master rabbi. An uncle of Jesus, (perhaps a brother of Joseph in the Essenes), he was called *Nicodemus.* Jesus is reported to have had a conversation with *Nicodemus* wherein Jesus said, "Why do you ask these questions? Are you not a master of Israel?" We are not sure what this means, but it seems significant.

194

After the Crucifixion, although not recorded in the Bible, *Nicodemus* resigned his position as chief rabbi at the Jerusalem Boys School and joined the close followers of Jesus. He was designated among the seventy original disciples of Jesus.

After the life of *Nicodemus,* we find this soul reentering the stream of Christian history with a powerfully karmic life as the reforming Pope, *Gregory I,* called *the Great.* Born of a wealthy family, he became involved in public affairs and was appointed a prefect of Rome. He then turned his life toward piety and became a Benedictine monk, building several monasteries with his own money. In connecting *Gregory* to *Nicodemus,* we are reminded that Benedict was formerly John the Baptist, who was loved and greatly admired by *Nicodemus,*

---

[44] The biblical story of *Nehemiah* is essential reading for a full comprehension of the nature of the progress revealed in this study.

having received John's baptism, in that former life in Jerusalem.

The Church of Rome was stabilized and reformed under the able leadership of *Gregory*. After he was elected Pope in 590, he reformed the clergy, liturgy and Church practices. Promoting "plainsong," the Gregorian chant, he expanded the influence of the Church by foreign missionary activity. It was *Gregory* who sent Augustine with a small band of Benedictine monks to evangelize England. Augustine, the first Archbishop of Canterbury, was also formerly one of the seventy of the early Church.

Pope Gregory I
(c. 540—March 12, 604)   *Pope Gregory VII (Hildebrand)*
                                     (1020—1085)

Gregory the Great is considered a doctor of the Church. He may have been the most able Pope in Church history. In an interesting karmic return, in his next incarnation, this soul again became Pope as the reforming Italian "firebrand," the Benedictine monk *Hildebrand*, who was *Pope Gregory VII*.

Hildebrand joined the Benedictines at an early age. As a valued secretary and administrator, he served more than one Pope, until he himself was elected Pope in 1073. In comparing the lives of *Hildebrand* and *Gregory I*, we must recall that the Holy Roman Empire was on the rise under the Saxon kings. The spirit of the times was one of great conflict between church and state. There was also pressure of invasion from Italy, France and central Europe—from the Magyars in the East and from the Normans. This soul, the former *Nehemiah*, grand magistrate of the Persian empire, was back in his karmic element of political infighting. Justice cannot be done to the story of *Hildebrand* in this short space; a careful study of his life is highly recommended.

Gregory VII began as Pope by sending out edicts of reform. Although his moral energy was strong, it probably never occurred to him that the very idea of the Church as an organized Papal state—not a theme taught by Jesus, or believed by any of the first apostles—could have been an anachronistic energy left over from his ancient Persian karma.

In researching the life of *Gregory VII*, we notice that he excommunicated the German Roman Emperor Henry IV and waited for him to beg for forgiveness. These maneuvers contributed to civil war among the northern German princes and dukes. *Gregory*, no doubt, was trying to do his best to reform, protect and strengthen the Church. The psychic energy of his persona and the trials of the times are neatly transferred into the life of *Martin Luther*.

196

Martin Luther
(Nov. 10, 1483—1546)

Martin Luther, after whom the Lutheran Church was founded, is one of the major leaders of Christianity and of Western civilization. He began life in a humble family. With natural talent, he entered the University of Erfurt at the age of 18. At first he studied law but, after a close encounter with death, he turned to religion. He joined an Augustinian order in Erfurt and was ordained in 1507. Becoming a lecturer in moral philosophy in 1511, he received his doctorate in theology and a professorship of scripture.

Martin Luther's life story can be measured by the degree of sincerity with which he upheld the moral principles of spirituality in his advocacy. After a trip to the Vatican in 1510, *Luther* was deeply distressed by corruption among Church clerics, which included the practice of the open sale of indulgences—forgiveness of sin for a price. Later the Pope of that time, Leo X, openly allowed a campaign of indulgences, as a revenue-gathering tactic, offering the unlimited forgiveness of sins for a price through a traveling emissary. *Luther* countered by posting his famous 95 theses to the door of the church in Wittenberg.

Luther's 95 theses were quickly copied and circulated around Europe, precipitating a political crisis. *Luther* was offered political support against the Pope by some of the German princes. It is a long story, but eventually *Luther* was excommunicated. In some ways, his story is a reversal of the *Hildebrand* scenario. *Luther* tried to reform the Church from within, but to no avail. It is unlikely that he intended to break up the power of the central Church.

Nelson Rockefeller
Medici-Rockefeller Connection

Pope Leo X   *Nelson Rockefeller*
(Dec. 11, 1475—Dec. 1, 1521) *(July 8, 1908—Jan. 26, 1979)*

Pope Leo X, scion of the Medici Family, was Pope from 1513 to 1521. His soul reincarnated in the United States as *Nelson Rockefeller*, grandson of American oil magnate John D. Rockefeller. He served as assistant secretary of state, governor of New York, and unelected vice president of the United States under President Gerald Ford. A patron of the arts, *Nelson Rockefeller* was unable to read unassisted due to severe dyslexia. This disability was never revealed to the general public, an indication of the social power this family held.

Thus, one branch of the European Medici clan reincarnated in the Rockefeller family of New York. Many such former aristocracies still expect to own the world, continuing to consciously strive for ultimate ownership or rulership through insider control of public institutions, including the world banking systems. Such archaic feudal pretensions involve the remnant monetary aristocracies of the world. Although these efforts are not likely to succeed in the long-run, clandestine activities of this nature can greatly disrupt democratic social evolution.

For further disclosure of Rockefeller family designs for world rulership and ownership, it is recommended that you find Gary

Allen's *The Rockefeller File,* published in 1976. It includes a list of Rockefeller family business trusts and foundations and reveals the part they have played in the creation of a present-day blueprint for the new world order—under a one-world, paramilitary, corporate monetary system. Where else could the internal drive for this type of control come, but from a karmic repetition of past-life assumptions of authority and prerogative? The Medici live.

Teilhard de Chardin
Jesuit Scientist

From the perspective of a student of Akashic history, a study of the past lives of *Father Pierre Teilhard de Chardin,* Jesuit Priest, paleontologist and mystical cosmologist, is very informative. He is one of the great souls; although not yet a spiritual master, he is a fourth-degree initiate. He is one the highest evolved fifth-ray leaders on the path of the ray of science.

Born in France in 1881, *Pierre Teilhard de Chardin* was raised by Christian parents. His father introduced him to a love of nature and science and to the hobby of artifact collecting; his mother, who was religious, nurtured his love of humanity and nature. You are invited to study the writings and life of this great soul, who continues to be an inspiration to millions.

A natural scholar with a religious temperament, *Teilhard* entered the Jesuit order in 1899. He received a doctorate in science and eventually became a full-time lecturer at the Institut Catholique in Paris. After his acceptance of the theory of natural evolution led to his dismissal from this position, he traveled to China, where he spent over twenty years as a professional paleontologist.

With deep loyalty and determination, *Teilhard* maintained his solidarity with the Church. Nevertheless, he became one of the greatest Catholic mystical-scientific cosmologists. His devotion to Christ and the Church was characteristic of his lifelong dedication to the philosophical union between matter and spirit. The fact that the Church, and his order, refused to allow him to publish his form of scientific mysticism during his lifetime did not deter his efforts.

Pierre Teilhard's teachings were later published in *The Phenomenon of Man*, *The Divine Milieu*, *The Future of Man*, *Hymn of the Universe*, and *Christianity and Evolution*. His grand ideation embraced the unity of God in the midst of diversity, as one supreme God who could be known as nature in body, spirit and soul. He tied his mystic vision together with a cosmic perspective that included material evolution.

Teilhard's thought, which went beyond Catholic theology, presented an understanding that may, in truth, be a gift to the Roman Catholic Church—when its membership is able to receive it. As is often the case in the mission of an arhat, the collective body of humanity, as well as his own immediate group, is offered the potential for new vision or for a new beginning, or at least a door out of darkness. The arhat is capable of imprinting the results of his spiritual struggle on the greater collective in a way that is much stronger and deeper than the influence of any other soul. The work of *Pierre Teilhard de Chardin* is considered by many as the basis for a new integrative theology for the Catholic Church at the end of this age.

We find a clear linkage between *Teilhard* and two important former lives in the West. This great soul is a reincarnation of one of the major figures of modern philosophy, the seventeenth century French philosopher, scientist-mathematician, *Rene Descartes*. This may be surprising to those who are not familiar with the life and work of *Rene Descartes*; however, after some preliminary study, this connection should be easy to discern.

Pierre Teilhard de Chardin
(May 1, 1881—April 10, 1955)

Rene Descartes
(Mar. 31, 1596—Feb. 11, 1650)

Similarities abound between the lives of *Pierre Teilhard de Chardin* and *Rene Descartes*. For example, *Descartes* served voluntarily in the military for more than one campaign. *Teilhard,* although a priest, served in the French militia as a stretcher bearer in the first World War. A humble corporal, he was decorated with the Medaille Militaire and with the Legion d'Honneur. Both *Teilhard* and *Descartes* had experience as soldiers, both became advocates for the new vision of science and both were dedicated to reconstructing mediaeval views in a natural light. The intellectual work of both was suppressed by the ignorance and fear of lesser minds. Like that of *Teilhard*, some of *Descartes'* work was published posthumously.

Neither of these great philosophers turned against the Church. In fact, the specter of the Inquisition's condemnation of Galileo's defense of Copernicus successfully intimidated *Descartes*. After the excommunication of Galileo, *Descartes* suppressed publication of his own work, *The World,* in which he took the same position as had Galileo. This was a severe karmic test. Courage must take a stand, but wisdom need not suffer fools. Thus, the karmic choice is always a personal one. History might have been different, at least in terms of the power of the Church over scholarship, if *Descartes* had published in defense of Galileo. We can reflect on this question but we must not judge it.

Works of *Rene Descartes* include *Meditations of First Philosophy*, written in France and published the year Isaac Newton (who lived again as Albert Einstein) was born. Several of *Descartes'* other works were written in Holland, where he traveled to secure greater intellectual freedom. These include *Discourse on Method: a Preface to Dioptrics, Meteors, and Geometry*, *Principles of Philosophy*, *The Passions of the Soul*, *Notes Against a Program* and his uncompleted work *Directions of the Mind,* published posthumously in 1701.

Rene Descartes was a reincarnation of the same soul who was the ninth century Irish Christian-theologian and Neoplatonist, *John Scotus Erigena*. His life is important for a better understanding of the evolution of Western philosophical thought.

John Scotus Erigena was one of the most influential philosophers of ninth century Christian Europe. It can be said that he broadcast a light out of the closet of collective darkness—a light that many would follow. The thought and intellectual lifework of

Erigena played a tutorial role in the development of creative thinking for such philosophers as Giordano Bruno and Benedict de Spinoza, as well as for *Descartes*, himself. Such souls, who work as teachers from the higher dimensions of life, and who are able to function creatively from the higher levels as well, seem to recognize and draw upon one another's inspiration.

John Scotus Erigena
(c. 810—877)

John Scotus Erigena emerged out of the mire of mediaeval thinking as an important contributor to Christian ideation. He contributed many important mystical principles that increased European collective understanding of higher spirituality. Spending most of his creative life in France as head of the court school of Charles II, *Erigena* studied and translated the complete works of Dionysius, the sixth century pseudo-Areopagite. Inspired by this Neoplatonic work, which included esoteric teachings on the hierarchies of the angel kingdom, *Erigena* continued in the Neoplatonic tradition and created his own original work. His *Periphyseon*, or *De divisione naturae* (On the Division of Nature) includes thoughts that can be considered philosophical parents to *Father Teilhard's* work—thoughts such as "the fulfillment of God in his theophany, which neither creates nor is created" and "as a principle of nature, the return of all things to God." *Erigena's* work was condemned by Pope Honorius III at Sens in 1225 and all copies were ordered to be burned.

The deeper and anonymous origins of this soul's past-life learning are as a priest and teacher in early China, Sumeria and Egypt, as well as a Grecian student, brother and teacher in the academy of Pythagoras. However the most important and interesting link for all these lives is in China, where *Teilhard* spent many years studying and teaching. Many of the Neoplatonic nature mystics of the Western traditions have had important lives linked—sometimes only by the common appreciation of a teacher or teaching—with former lives in the Taoist tradition. In fact, almost all Western theological positions have been expressed, in one form or another, in early Chinese traditions, as well as throughout Asia in Hindu and Buddhist traditions.

Alice Bailey
Tibetan Connection

This study is intended to expand our understanding of the principle of soul group cohesion on the mental plane of consciousness. Those souls who are working to develop spiritual capacities on the mental plane for use on earth are drawn together. By association, these souls tend to become part of a universal college in higher dimensions. In these schools of higher learning, different group formations offer specialization in much the same way that colleges on earth are established within a university.

The formation of spiritual colleges is timeless and ageless. Souls go there to learn from higher teachers as well as to teach newer students. This type of spiritual activity takes place continuously in the higher realms during both waking and sleeping life, and even more intensely between lives.

In all schools of higher learning spiritual masters sponsor lines of discipleship. From such lines emerge specialist teachers, who are then designated to be the elder teachers of a particular school. Spiritual sponsorship and the accelerated spiritual growth at such centers of learning helps active students increase their conscious access to progressively greater levels of spirit.

One or more of these elder teachers from the higher spheres occasionally incarnates on earth with a mission to make a contribution that will affect the mental fabric of the entire world collective. As is natural to such souls, and according to the spiritual karma of their particular specialty focus, these elder teachers may establish a center of learning in the physical world. Such a gathering inevitably reflects a group incarnation, a gathering of souls belonging to a specialty group from one of the inner colleges of higher learning.

The following soul identifications should be contemplated gently and absorbed slowly; this information is intended as food for intuition.

The life and thought of *Plotinus* of Rome should be compared with the acknowledged father of Taoism, *Lao Tsu*. This ancient Chinese mystic's insights were collected in approximately 500 B.C. in a book known as the *Tao Te Ching*. The insights of *Plotinus* were collected around A.D. 275 in a book called *The Enneads*, published in Rome by his student Porphyry.

Lao Tsu (Li Erh)   *Plotinus*
(Sixth century B.C.)   *(AD 204-270)*

Lao Tsu and *Plotinus* share the same inner being. The profound enlightenment and inner gentleness of these two mystic philosophers is immediately apparent. This soul has now become a spiritual master.

Because *Plotinus* established an academy in Rome with open doors, his soul karma includes a social invitation to Western public awareness and involvement. The karmic connection of *Plotinus* to the West allowed him to more easily reenter the stream of Western collective consciousness, this time by opening an academy of spiritual training in New York City in the first half of the twentieth century. This school, an outgrowth of the international theosophical movement, was called the Arcane School.

This master chose a former disciple, then incarnated as *Alice Bailey*, who is also a former teacher of Western theology, to serve as the "lens" of distribution. Thus, the work of the Arcane School was sponsored, introduced, mantled, shepherded, protected and edited by a star of Western and Eastern philosophical and religious development. This particular master, a father of early Neoplatonism and of Chinese philosophical mysticism, is now known as the Master Djwhal Khul (The Tibetan).

The teachings of Master Djwhal Khul include such subjects as esoteric psychology, astrology and white magic. The purpose of this teaching is thought purification. The teaching of the Arcane School is a form of esoteric philosophical mysticism, openly presenting mystical and occult insights that for centuries were considered secrets. This open presentation by a master is intended to help students from varied cultural backgrounds avoid the psychic entrapments of shamanist beliefs and folk-religions. The specialized work of this school was intended to lift collective thought concerning all forms of occult studies to a more spiritual focus.[45]

Philosophical and occult mysticism, as a religious specialty, developed in various later Mesopotamian-Grecian mystery schools and religious training academies. Some of the same elder souls are interconnected, through reincarnation, with spiritual development in several world regions/religions, including Sumerian, Egyptian, Hindu, Chinese, Buddhist, Zoroastrian, and eventually organized Christian religion.

207

The story continues to unfold, but who was the Tibetan's disciple; who was *Alice Bailey*?

Chuang Tsu, a follower of *Lao Tsu*, used a natural and charming style to comment on *The Way of Lao Tsu*. His writing is considered among the most valuable of the ancient Chinese classics. Perhaps more important for the soul of the reincarnating *Chuang Tsu* was his spiritual-magnetic attraction to *Plotinus* and to his

---

[45] A purified form of philosophical mysticism, including white magic, evolved in the West under the influence of Zoroaster, now also a spiritual master (but not yet a master in his earth life as Zoroaster). The general influence of philosophical-mystical purification in the West—in Judaism, Islam and in Christendom—is due, in great part, to the profound influence of Zoroaster. This master is now responsible for guiding the future of Christian Russia.

school in Rome. Here we find the life of a philosopher known as *Iamblichus*, the Syrian.

Chuang Tsu (Zhuangzi)
(Fourth century B.C.)

Iamblichus
(250—330)

The life of *Iamblicus* is not easily placed in clear perspective because he was both vilified and idolized for centuries. He was considered by many to be *the* authority on Neoplatonism, both Arabic and Christian, for over two centuries. The two most important connecting lives that we will choose for this meditation are *Iamblichus* and his next life as *Albertus Magnus*.

Is this the same soul? That is the important question. You are advised to approach this meditation, after proper biographical research, as if this were the same soul, regardless of appearances. Then study, by attuning to a higher intuitive flow, possible karmic connection and the spiritual growth patterns involved.

With careful reflection, we conclude that *Iamblichus* was not that spiritually "high." He was a specialist—as was *Albertus Magnus* who, with careful examination, can also be found to be lacking in higher forms of spiritual purity and enlightenment. However, within their respective personal and karmic conditions, each was a magnificent teacher. Tens of thousands of philosophy students, if not millions, owe this old soul a spiritual debt of gratitude for his contribution to general psychic-spiritual upliftment. While the fabric of our collective mental potential is woven by the work of many souls, this soul is one of the great craftsmen for that effort and, thereby, a world-class elder disciple of the God of light.

Albertus Magnus(the Great) was a medieval German theologian and scholastic philosopher. Interested in the early stages of scientific theory, he studied many sources of knowledge—especially the Greeks Plato and Aristotle, and the later Neoplatonists. During his lifetime, *Albertus* was considered a greater authority than his more famous student, Thomas Aquinas. *Albertus* was an authority on Aristotelian philosophy and was responsible for the realist approach that became the foundation of the theology of Aquinas—which, in turn, became (some may say unfortunately) the theological basis of Catholicism.

Albertus held the chair of theology at the University of Paris (again a reincarnational French-Chinese connection) and was founder of the University of Cologne. He was responsible for collecting and writing over forty volumes—a veritable encyclopedia of the extant knowledge of his time. Called the *doctor universalis* (universal doctor) by his students and followers, *Albertus* was finally officially recognized as a doctor of the Church and made a saint in 1931. In that same year, *Alice Bailey* was invited to establish a teaching center in Europe on the Swiss-Italian border at Ascona, on Lake Maggiore.

209

Albertus Magnus   *Alice A. Bailey*
(c. 1200—Nov. 15, 1280)   *(June 16, 1880—Dec. 15, 1949)*

Alice Ann (La Trobe-Bateman) Bailey was born to a wealthy class-conscious family in Manchester, England at the end of the

Victorian era. Her life is one of the more fascinating stories to arise out of the theosophical movement. You may find it worthwhile to review the *Unfinished Autobiography of Alice Bailey*, first published in 1951. However, there is much more to her story than these ruminations of a sixty-seven-year-old woman.

All her life this soul's feminine persona was torn between two worlds. She lived on a social bridgeway between changing times of upheaval in religious tradition and public mores. *Bailey* was an intelligent, sensitive woman, both submissive (as was required by her social era) and aggressive (as called forth by an amazing inner depth of intellect). That a woman was called to do the type of work she did emphasizes the genius of her spiritual masters. Her feminine energy reflected the needs of the present era; the age of Aquarius must bring the balance of a feminine influence to all levels of human leadership.

During the course of her life, *Bailey's* personal karma was greatly speeded up. An upper-class British woman, she volunteered to serve as a Christian missionary with the British army in India. (We recall that *Albertus Magnus*, originally an aristocrat, preached the crusades.) *Bailey's* personal life led her away from a position of social elitism, although she may have compensated for this loss by clinging to intellectual elitism.

Bailey had a personal struggle adjusting to life as a woman. She fought suicidal tendencies during her childhood and depression during her teen and young-adult years. A form of Victorian-era repression-hysteria overwhelmed her at age twenty. She experienced a nervous breakdown when faced with romantic choices, while serving as a missionary nurse in a British soldiers hospital in India.

Bailey's choice in men reflected personal inexperience and lack of confidence. She fell in love with one of her patients, a British army private, whom she personally converted to the Christian evangelistic faith. She eventually married him, after he was sent to America by her family to gain social position by becoming an Episcopal priest. They had three children together. Due to her background and temperament, her personal life was very difficult, and her marriage turned out to be the most difficult. Her husband beat her often and would not help her in any way in the house work. Although she claimed that he did not misbehave in other ways, he eventually abandoned her, and she had to raise the children on her own.

Brought by circumstances to unreservedly embrace working class life—probably in her best karmic interest—she worked for awhile in a sardine canning factory in Los Angeles after her marriage failed. Through this time of personal difficulty, she was forced to experience the pain as well as challenge of single-parenthood and the pride of self-sufficiency. All this led eventually to her experiencing a sense of normalcy in a woman's self reliance. For one who had been a monk and scholastic priest many times before, these were important karmic challenges.

When *Bailey* was thirty-five years old, in 1915, her life took a new direction. She made acquaintance with two British ladies who lived near her in Los Angeles and who were theosophists. Once *Bailey* opened the door to her intellectual-mental potential, she discovered she was a natural philosopher and teacher. Finding that a full grasp of Helena Blavatsky's *Secret Doctrine* was a necessity, *Bailey* enjoyed the academic-spiritual challenge and easily mastered the field. She appreciated the mental expansion and psychic opening that theosophy was intended to address. In fact, she found herself able to teach classes in theosophy in a matter of weeks, so like a sponge was her inner capacity. For example, she taught a class in 1915 on Annie Besant's *A Study in Consciousness*, while staying only six pages ahead of her class. This is what is meant by natural spiritual capacity.

Bailey's intellectual and personal lives were on different wave lengths.[46] She could, however, consciously tune into either of her worlds—the emotional/personal or the mental/intellectual—and was out-spoken against any form of unconscious spirit channeling. Her natural capacity to tune into higher frequencies of thought

---

[46] The *Alice Bailey* study is a good example of the two fields of persona and mind, somewhat divided. Although sometimes such a condition is inevitable due to personal limitation, a mind-self and feeling-self separation is not a spiritual ideal. Many mystics believe that the way to spiritual wholeness is to merge mind and heart into one unified whole. As both mental and emotional awareness becomes united in an inclusive soul awareness, a spiritual form of higher intelligence emerges.

resulted in her discovery of an ability to recall lessons delivered in the inner halls of learning. She termed this recall "listening to the master." She was not particularly open to the general subject of visual clairvoyance—which she, herself, did not possess—although she did practice a form of mental clairvoyance.

Bailey wrote down the lessons she received telepathically. She and her new husband Foster Bailey, who was a leader in American theosophy and with whom she had moved to New York, gathered the lessons over a period of years. These writings have since been collected into many volumes of esoteric instruction. As far as our studies are concerned, there is no reason to doubt that these lessons were received from Master Djwhal Khul. *Bailey* has said much about the channeling of these teachings and their publication in English. Apparently these books were part of a planned spiritual mission, something the masters and their disciples wished to have distributed in the world. Due to this sponsorship, *Bailey's* telepathic writing was mantled by spiritual protection.

The writings of *Alice Bailey* and Master Djwhal Khul will likely continue to affect the spiritual-intellectual milieu of this planet for centuries to come. They include such titles as *Initiations, Human and Solar*; *A Treatise on Cosmic Fire; The Consciousness of the Atom*; *The Light of the Soul*; *From Bethlehem to Calvary*; *From Intellect to Intuition*; *A Treatise on White Magic*; *The Destiny of the Nations*; *Education in the New Age;* and *A Treatise on the Seven Rays*. If you are up to it, a careful study of these books is a good way to deepen your comprehension of the field of religious/esoteric science and philosophy.

Toyohiko Kagawa
Christian Missionary to Japan

Toyohiko Kagawa was one of the great Christian evangelists and missionaries of the first half of the twentieth century. Although it may be confusing to some, this case has a great depth of beauty. Again, we are addressing the karmic complexity of the progression of a great soul, a spiritual arhat. A poet, novelist and writer of religious tracts, *Kagawa* dedicated his life to bringing a Christian mission of aid and enlightenment to the slums of Tokyo. He was a pacifist who advocated peoples' cooperatives, a form of Christian political populism that often made enemies in "Caesar's camp." Perhaps this is why his story is not well-known.

Toyohiko Kagawa's life was a gem of spiritual vision and insight. He "reached out to heaven" to bring the leadership and power of a great soul into practical application. At the beginning of World War II, when military ascendancy was winning the day worldwide, this lonely voice reflected one of the great lights then living on earth. His was clearly a voice for the kingdom of Christ on earth in opposition to impending worldwide imperialism.

Toyohiko Kagawa was the reincarnation of *Ignatius of Loyola*, founder of the Catholic order of the Jesuits.

213

Toyohiko Kagawa
(1888—1960)

Ignatius of Loyola
(1491— July 31, 1556)

Born to a noble Basque family near San Sebastian, Spain, *Ignatius of Loyola* received a good education. He served in the military, in service to the viceroy of Navarre. While recovering from a leg wound received in battle, he read a life of Christ that ignited, for the first time in his life, a spiritual spark. After this awakening, he dedicated himself to religious service. He set out on a pilgrimage to Jerusalem, stopping along the way at the Benedictine abbey of Montserrat in Catalonia, where he stayed for awhile. During this time, *Loyola* had many mystical experiences and "grounded" an enlightenment that had previously existed in his soul. He later developed a method of spiritual discipline based on his experiences during this period.

The conditions of a life, a time and a culture can greatly affect the vision and direction of one who is a great soul. It is the mission of the arhat to take the path before him and transform it to the best of his ability. This *Loyola* tried to do. One way to analyze his life's work is to realize that he worked with and within the Catholic social order of his day. If his life was a mission, it was a mission for the Church. In fact, because the forms of communal reformation *Loyola* and the Jesuits organized in their various missions were threatening to the Catholic militant aristocracy of their day, they had more enemies within the Church than without.

The work of a great soul always has an effect on a greater collective. Such work can manifest on any level—whether it be on the mental, the emotional or the cultural plane only, or on all planes of physical manifestation. These highly karmic souls carry the weight of the collective in making their karmic choices. They have the capacity and, therefore, the dharma to do their best to uplift the destiny of thousands of souls. This they do both in their inner and outer lives.

It is as if karmic angels watched over the incarnation of that great soul. Even for arhats, however, success is not guaranteed, and sometimes they make errors. As a principle, the higher world cannot interfere with their choices. What such a soul is able to accomplish in his lifetime defines the capacity of the greater collective. Thus, the life of an arhat represents a test of the readiness for spiritual help, or the worthiness of spiritual grace, of the greater body of people. In the case of *Ignatius of Loyola,* his collective group included all those who embraced Roman Catholicism at that time.

When a great soul receives support from others who respond to, or are called by, his mission, the whole collective gains forward spiritual momentum. This is an indirect means by which society can align with its own best good. The responsiveness of a people to a spiritual leader is important to that people. A true path can be chosen and a new vision actualized through the influence of an arhat. If no help or desire for transformation is forthcoming from the general collective, or a specialized group within that collective, the arhat will likely experience his or her life as a failure. If a chosen mission of one of these great ones falters, then so goes the future direction of that collective—until another arhat or saint or initiate is sent to show the way.

Ignatius of Loyola was one such as these, caught in the tides and rip-tides of a changing age. His life was essentially a socio-religious experiment; the full spiritual potential of his soul did not manifest in that life. You should take special care in reviewing *Loyola's* life. Because of the tremendous controversy surrounding his life, it is advisable to study diverse biographical sources.

215

Tertullian
(160—220)

We find that this soul was a reincarnation of Christendom's third century apostle, *Tertullian* of Carthage, who was one of the greatest organizing fathers of the early Christian church. A meditation on some of the karmic choices and religious expressions of

Tertullian can help you better understand the complexity of the spiritual-psychic countercurrents that ran from *Tertullian* through to the life of *Ignatius Loyola* and then into the life of *Toyohiko Kagawa*.

Born in Carthage at the midpoint of the second century, *Quintus Septimius Florens Tertullianus*, called *Tertullian*, became one of the most important theologians of Christian antiquity. Of fiery temperament and great talent, *Tertullian* was a natural leader. He trained for the law and practiced advocacy in Rome for many years. After he converted to Christianity at the age of 37, he gave the full power of his sharp intelligence to the cause of Christian advocacy. A natural first-ray soul, he became dissatisfied with the existing form of early Christianity, and started his own group called the *Tertullianists*. Because of his free and lascivious early life, *Tertullian* became somewhat of an extremist in advocating spiritual discipline. His followers may have found his disciplines to be hard, but *Tertullian's* natural brilliance never faltered.

Tertullian's writings greatly influenced the development of Christian theology, affecting the thinking and feeling of many generations of later Christians.

Albert Schweitzer
Evolution of Saint Peter

In this study, we present four famous lives of the soul who was *Simon Peter*, disciple of Jesus. This soul is also one of the most important "pattern" arhats for the general community of the Christian church. His progress exemplifies the process of "grounding," or bringing to earth, spiritual potential. In each of these progressive lives, this soul is experiencing the accumulative spiritual capacity of all proceeding lives. In each life, he manifested a new level of initiation, one after the other. He may have achieved these levels in previous lives, but he chose to reproduce each of the levels again.

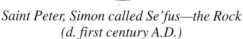

Saint Peter, Simon called Se'fus—the Rock
(d. first century A.D.)

A meditation on the life of *Simon Peter.* must be approached with gentleness and humility. Called *Saint Peter* by the Church, this soul has been shrouded by a cloak of religious idealism that has inadvertently projected some historical misrepresentations. His person has been elevated over time to the position of a supreme icon in the hearts and minds of millions. The startling effect of this is that a direct approach to his life study is blocked by many subtle layers of astral assumptions. Astral assumptions can have an effect on lower mental levels of the Akashic Records, blocking direct perception. This influence has been applied to the Records over a period of many centuries by religious devotees thinking or wishing something to be true.

Simon Peter was called *Se'fus* by Jesus (Se'fus means "rock" in Greek). *Peter* was a strong, intelligent, sensitive, fiery-tempered, Aramaic/Judean fisherman, who lived and worked on the shores of Lake Galilee. In that life, he was called to discipleship by Jesus, for a public mission that led to the creation of a new religious-based social community.

In his life as *Simon Peter,* he expressed the emotional, mental and spiritual transformation and commitment characteristic of the first degree of initiation. Other great souls surrounding Jesus in that life in Palestine were James the Less (the Brother of Jesus), John the Baptist and Rabbi Gamaliel.[47]

We learn from the Bible story of Luke that it was *Peter* who first voiced the intuitive insight that Jesus was the Messiah. Jesus said, "The spirit has revealed this to you, *Peter.*" *Peter* was also present at the vision of the transfiguration while Jesus prayed in the garden. There, he saw two archangels speaking to Jesus. This was later interpreted by *Peter* as a vision of Moses and Elijah.

It was *Peter* who had the vision of Jesus coming to him across the water. This dream-vision was later interpreted by devotees who heard the story as Jesus "walking on water." The term "walking on water" meant that Jesus appeared out of the invisible realm to speak with and comfort *Peter.* In this vision, Jesus held out his hand and took *Peter* out of his physical body and into the spirit realms.

Peter had hundreds of previous lives in every land and major culture on earth. Most of these lives were not historically famous; one of interest, however, was as a loyal friend of Pharaoh Akhenaten of Egypt, named *Parenefer.*[48] Slowly, over millennia, *Peter* developed a

---

[47] Gamaliel, a grandson of the great Jewish theologian Hillel, was a Pharisee and head of the Jerusalem Boys School; he was a former teacher of Saul of Tarsus, who in turn was the founder of Christian biblical theology.

[48] All of the above named great souls, except John the Baptist, had former lives with the Arhat Pharaoh Akhenaten; they had all formerly engaged in building the city Akhetaten (City of the One God) in Egypt in 1340 B.C.

refined soul capacity in relation to earth lives. At least a third-degree initiate in his life as *Peter*, he is now a fourth-degree initiate. From the four lives presented here, it is evident that this great soul has come to lift the conscious alignment of humanity out of the old spiritual paradigm into a new relationship with the divine world. Every step he has taken successfully in the world has "baptized" the human collective with a new potential of spirit and in the direction of a New Age.[49]

The twelve disciples were chosen as official witnesses, but were also guided to become an organized core for prayer and wisdom, around which a community could develop. The spiritual methods taught by Jesus and his early disciples invited God in as a great act of faith—assuming "God With Us." Human authoritarianism was not a legitimate factor in that first community of the "kingdom of the Way." Calling themselves "followers of the Way," the early Christians organized a communal society and retained their independent fishing and agricultural way of life. Personal freedom with responsibility to others was a basic premise of their spiritual understanding. The understanding of "God With Us" in community, and a belief in resurrection to immortal life, were at the core of their faith. Dedicated to pure mystical theocracy, the early disciples waited daily on the guidance of God, and trusted in the protective mantle of the Holy Spirit.

This earliest form of Christian community was inspired by the Essenes; its beliefs and practices were validated and clarified by

---

[49] The *Book of Luke* in the Bible expresses the general story of the life of Jesus and the responsibility that was given to *Peter* and the disciples. We must realize that the clear admonition by Jesus not to write anything down in any authoritarian form is not made clear in the Bible—otherwise how would the Bible exist? "The Word of God would be written in their hearts and minds." Jesus was not a fan of written rules, or the making of sacred laws in written form into a religious fetish. Thus, he instructed no one to write. The "letters," the four gospels, reporting the events of the life of Christ, although held sacred, must be understood as having historical value. These collected writings are not a transmission of authority from God to any man or institution. For example, the saying "God is a jealous God" simply meant that God kept all of the authority and gave away none to any individual or institution. *Peter*, although intelligent and capable, was dedicated by the example of Jesus to the "way of spirit," and did not write in that life.

Jesus. After his death, the community came under extreme persecution and was scattered. *Peter* stayed for a while near Galilee with many of the early followers but, after the persecutions increased, he and a few others escaped to Damascus, Syria. They eventually made their way to a safe-haven in Alexandria, Egypt, hoping to create a safer place for the remnant core community. Alexandria is where *Peter* died, not Rome.

This great soul reincarnated a hundred years later in Athens, although that was not his first time in Greece. His name in that life was *Clement*.

Born to a wealthy family, *Clement* received a fine education in Platonic philosophy, including complete intellectual immersion in Gnostic scriptures. At a relatively early age, feeling the pull of spirit, he converted to Christianity, then a vital religious faith in that region.

As *Clement of Alexandria*, this soul's full intellectual capacity emerged. He became one of the first great Gnostic fathers. This life was characteristic of the work of a fully developed second-degree initiate. Considered by some to be the founder of Neoplatonism, *Clement* continues to have an important influence on evolving Western philosophy.

Clement of Alexandria　　　*Emanuel Swedenborg*
(c. 150—c. 215)　　　*(Jan. 29, 1688—Mar. 29, 1772)*

In a later European life, although not his next life, this great leader was born in Sweden, in a group repetition of an earlier,

3000 B.C. Sumerian life. He was trained as a scientist, developing his intellectual capacities to a highly advanced level. His name in that life was *Emanuel Swedenborg*. It was a life that reflected a highly complex karma.

Emanuel Swedenborg was a world-renowned scientist and mystic. In 1745, after a lifetime of scientific work in which he won acclaim as a theorist, he experienced a spiritual illumination that radically changed his view of life. His earlier study of mathematics, mechanics and physics had come from a deep personal interest in cosmology and theology. After his illumination at the age of sixty, *Swedenborg* began a second career as a seer and interpreter of the spiritual world, of which he claimed direct vision. Using the religious language of his day, he wrote long treatises on the spirit world, in the form of divinely revealed interpretations of the Bible.

An in-depth review of the mystical thought of *Swedenborg* (beyond our scope here) will reveal the remarkable karmic continuity between *Simon Peter* and *Swedenborg*. *Swedenborg's* religious speculations also represent a completion of the work of *Clement* in Christian gnosticism. *Swedenborg* stated that the proper approach to spiritual reality and God is through, rather than in rejection of, material nature.[50]

Swedenborg's life work is a reflection of the new enlightenment in Europe at that time. His visionary success as a witness to greater spiritual reality is characteristic of the accomplishment of a third-degree initiate. Although his work was an extension of

221

---

[50] An entire book of theology could be written on this theme; suffice it to say that this is the ageless theme of all theology. For example, the beliefs of the classic Chinese nature mystics, which were opposed by the social and material realism of the early Confucian school, reflect this concern should the focus of enlightened thought be on real life, or on spirit life? The theology of early Christianity reflected the concern of the division of spirit and matter. Early Zoroastrian belief, which influenced all later Mesopotamian religion including Judaism, was based on a premise of division of spirit and matter into hierarchies of good and evil. This was the great point of discussion; the Christian Church has argued the problem of the division of spirit and matter for centuries. Was Christ man or spirit? Do we embrace natural life or leave it?

that done by others—such as Benedict de Spinoza, Roger Bacon, Francis Bacon and Bruno—by all indications, his revelations were original visionary experiences and not based on direct study of the work of others. He was one of the first to open a door for popular study of theosophy, in much the same way that *Clement* legitimized Gnostic and Neoplatonic philosophy for early Christianity.

Swedenborg proclaimed prophetically that the archaic age was ending. Henceforth, he said, warfare between good and evil spirits would be played out on the earth plane. This notion was very Zoroastrian. In the light of the following two centuries of warfare, this was an astute prophecy. A new political age based on public representation began at that time, as exemplified by the birth of the American republic.

Swedenborg's spiritual ideas gave rise to a religious movement called the Church of New Jerusalem, and later to *Swedenborgian* societies. The *Swedenborgian* principles, which were taught by such groups, held enormous influence around the world, especially in Europe and America. In America, for example, *Swedenborg's* influence can be found among the nineteenth century New England transcendentalists, who included such leaders as Fuller, Alcott and Emerson.

If our theme is correct—that this soul was taking steps to reproduce each of the four great initiations, one life after another—then he had one more life to give. That life would be greater still, a life of Christian service in which he could demonstrate the highest gift a man can give: his life for his fellow man. Such a life of public service and self-sacrifice for others is often required of fourth-degree initiates.

This soul reincarnated again in the twentieth century. This would be a more Christian life in terms of service to humanity than any of his previous lives. In this next life, he became the brilliant German Kantian philosopher, Christian seminary theologian, Bach concert organist and medical missionary to French equatorial Africa, *Dr. Albert Schweitzer.*

Dr. Albert Schweitzer
(Jan. 14, 1875—Sept. 4, 1965)

Awarded the Nobel Peace Prize in 1952, *Dr. Albert Schweitzer* was one of the world's great Christian missionaries. A review of *Schweitzer's* youth and education reveals the karma of being born into a life of opportunity, in which he received a sound emotional and intellectual foundation.

He was born in the German territory of Upper Alsace, which became French after World War I. His father was a Lutheran pastor at Gunsbach. The young boy began organ lessons at his father's church at the age of five. He later became one of Europe's greatest Bach concert organists. This is important because music can heal and rebuild the emotional and mental bodies when they have been depleted. *Schweitzer* used music in his work as a Christian missionary and to heal the personal disassociation evident in at least two of his previous lives. *Swedenborg's* efforts to build an historical bridge from the Old Testament to the present day had been a waste of psychic energy. His attempts to introduce clairvoyance to the mind of modern man were also stressful.

The Lutheran chapel at Gunsbach, on occasion, served both Catholics and Lutherans, and the territory was bilingual. This tolerant social environment contributed greatly to young *Schweitzer's* emotional development, later so beautifully expressed in his writings and missionary work. His life theme, on which he built an integrated philosophy, came to him on a river trip in Africa: it was "reverence for life." This ideal, based on the premise of God as father of all life, included universal responsibility, acceptance, tolerance and especially reverence toward one's fellows. This theme fully embraced life on earth, in much the same way as did the teachings of Jesus.

Schweitzer attended the University at Strasbourg. In 1899, after studying in Paris and completing a dissertation on the philosophy of Immanuel Kant, he received his first doctorate in philosophy. Two years later, he completed the requirements for a doctorate in theology, at the College of Saint Thomas. This, according to his autobiography, allowed him to pursue his greatest love, that of preaching in church on Sunday and teaching in the seminary.

In 1906, *Schweitzer* published *The Quest for the Historical Jesus,* which gained him worldwide fame. It addressed the subject of a balance between history, archeology and religious assumption. He attempted to connect his mind and emotion with the life and teachings of Jesus. Successful or not, this effort was aimed at uplifting the collective.

It is difficult to say what effect the writing of *The Quest for the Historical Jesus* had on *Schweitzer*, but in 1906, against everyone's advice, he entered the medical school at Saint Thomas, determined to become a doctor of medicine so that he could do medical missionary work. His wife, whom he married in 1912, was also a scholar in her own right, trained in nursing. In 1913, they left for French equatorial Africa to establish a hospital for the poor and disenfranchised. This is the work that won him the Nobel Prize.

Schweitzer intended to share his time between hospital duties and his greatest love, writing. Leaving civilization behind gave the *Schweitzers* an opportunity to focus on their missionary ideals and on religious studies, free of frivolous social demands. In Europe, *Schweitzer* had been constantly called upon to give Bach organ recitals, mostly for rich, complacent people. He did not wish to live an irrelevant life, teaching principles to young men and women who would never fully appreciate or use them. He may have felt sickened by the excesses of modern civilization, a sentiment that often leads to spiritual awakening. He may also have been recovering from a partial nervous breakdown in his preceding life.

Albert Schweitzer was disturbed by the specter of continued warfare among Christian nations. He sensed a possible breakdown of civilization, which seemed to be approaching on every horizon. *Swedenborg,* we recall, taught about a coming world war that would descend out of the psychic realms onto earth, a final banishment of darkness that implied a breakdown of civilization. These thought forms generated by *Swedenborg* penetrated strongly into *Schweitzer's* mind.

There is a follow-up curio to this study. In the early 1960s, *Schweitzer* gave a speech in New York City in which he stated, "I apologize for not speaking better English; in my next life I will be an American." This prophetic statement, although perhaps meant as a joke, has come true. On occasion, such a great soul will live two or more lives in quick succession. This may be due to spiritual velocity, or a pull of spirit groundedness in earth, or may be a way for an older soul to pay off a last bit of karma to earth before taking time out for a few hundred years.

This soul reincarnated in the United States in the late 1960s. In this present, publicly anonymous life, he is of African American decent. A dedicated evangelistic Christian in his early teens, and an exceptional athlete, this young man excelled in academics and sports. He received a full financial scholarship to a major university. After completing medical school, he became a family practice doctor and part-time preacher. His life will bring aid and inspiration to many, especially among the black Christian community where he resides. Thus, this great one's soul influence is again helping to generate spiritual empowerment for a group of people in need.

Brother Lawrence
Christian Mysticism

Here, we have another example of the power of one whose karmic history is connected with the Bible. The temple priest *Zechariah* is mentioned at the beginning of Luke, in the New Testament.

According to the *Book of Luke,* during one of *Zechariah's* rounds of appointed service in the inner sanctuary of the temple, an angel called Gabriel appeared to him. This angel announced that *Zechariah's* wife, Elizabeth, who had until then been barren, would soon conceive a child. The couple had been praying fervently for a child. According to the Bible story, *Zechariah* was at first afraid of the apparition and hesitated. The angel told him that, because of this doubt, he would be made temporarily mute, unable to utter a word until the birth of the child. This male child, said the angel, would be called to the service of the Lord and was destined to become a great prophet. "God, the Lord of Israel, would go before him in the spirit and power of Elijah." That child became John the Baptist, cousin of Jesus of Nazareth.

Zechariah—Father of John the Baptist
(40 B.C.—20 A.D.)

This soul, the former *Zechariah*, was in that life a third-degree initiate, who had developed through many lives as a natural mystic of the spiritual path of the heart. It is interesting to trace his future incarnations after his participation in the great passion play of Christ. We find a magnetic pull to Christian mysticism. We find him again incarnating in the West as *Nicholas Herman,* known as *Brother Lawrence.*

Nicholas Herman, a Carmelite friar known as *Brother Lawrence,* wrote one of the most influential diaries of Christian mysticism, *The Practice of the Presence of God.* His work is an example of eighteenth century French Catholic mysticism in its most sane form. Without laying claim to any special powers, and with perfect humility, *Brother Lawrence* described the way of acknowledgment and acceptance of God in everyday life. The life of *Brother Lawrence* is an example of a saint who was in alignment with the all-encompassing, mystical temple of God. His work remains as one of the purest and clearest examples of mysticism in Christian history.

We find this humble and accomplished soul reincarnating in the United States in the twentieth century. Again in a life of service to a higher spiritual mission, he became the co-founder of Questhaven Retreat, near San Diego, California.

227

Brother Lawrence   *Lawrence G. Newhouse*
(1611—1672)   *(July 18, 1910—January 29, 1963)*

Lawrence Newhouse was born near Chicago, Illinois. Shortly after graduating from high school, he went to Los Angeles, where he began an apprenticeship in printing, a craft that would serve his life mission. At the age of twenty-three, he met and married a young woman named Mildred Arlene Sechler, called Flower.

Flower Newhouse, prior to marrying Lawrence, had a fully developed writing and public speaking career. From the age of fifteen, she had been an accomplished public speaker, earning a living and supporting her mother and sister by lecturing and giving classes on various metaphysical subjects. She spoke openly about her clairvoyance, which she had possessed from childhood. Besides teaching about higher metaphysical principles, her talks included commentary on her inner visions of angels and the hidden workings of the devic and angel kingdoms. For the purpose of this study, it is interesting that *Lawrence*, who had been the recipient of an angel message in his biblical life, was the companion of one whose life-calling was an open conversation with the angelic world.

After their marriage, Flower and *Lawrence* worked faithfully together, recognizing a special mission to broadcast truth and to create a spiritual retreat center. The result of their life work is a magnificent, 640-acre nature sanctuary, Questhaven Retreat, near San Diego, California, which attracts people from all over the world. The *Newhouse* legacy also includes the retreat's Church of the Holy Quest, which continues to hold Sunday church services, and the Christward Ministry, which continues to publicize a New Age transformational teaching in the form of a unique expression of esoteric Christian mysticism.

The testimony to *Lawrence Newhouse's* life by those who knew him reflects a similar personality—with respect to spiritual strength, stability and character—to that of *Brother Lawrence*. In fact, as *Lawrence Newhouse,* this soul worked to build his dream retreat as a contribution to a future transformed and uplifted Christianity. His primary personal expression in all aspects of his work was that of joy in service to God.

The Reverend Billy Graham
Missionary to the World

This study emphasizes the wonder of the soul's journey from life to life. No matter how much understanding or enlightenment is achieved during one life, the soul must start over and learn it once again in each new life. Each life is a unique creation. Each life has a new physical body, a new emotional body and a new mental body. As we have discussed before, a personality lives only once. That person moves from the arena of this life into his reward in the afterlife.

The phrase "the hope for salvation" is the essence of the spiritual message that the *Reverend Billy Graham* has been broadcasting worldwide for over fifty years. His Christian evangelistic ministry and crusade have touched the lives of millions of people in every culture on earth. His ministry, now converted to the electronic media, is able to broadcast directly to millions of people simultaneously via satellite television.

Billy Graham   Bartolome de Las Casas
(Nov. 7, 1918—)   (1474—1566)

Two former lives of this soul, who is likely a first-degree initiate with a special dispensation of "Holy Spirit" magnetism, define a complex progression that matches the energy, commitment and call-to-mission that is evident in *Billy Graham's* life. In a life in American Hispanola, he was *Bartolome de Las Casas*, a Spanish aristocrat and former owner of a slave plantation, who experienced a conversion of spirit and became a Christian social reformer of noble character and purpose.

Bartolome de Las Casas, who came from an elite Spanish-French aristocratic family, was involved in trade negotiation and plantation building during his early years. He later became an outspoken, unrestrainable missionary who stood up against slavery. When the Indians of Hispanola and Cuba were reduced to slavery and worked to death without remorse, a great illumination touched the heart of *de Las Casas.* He had been involved in the trade and had owned slaves but, unlike the other slave owners, he treated his slaves benevolently. However, this was not enough.

De Las Casas was unable to resist the internal call to spiritual conversion that led him to a life of service and to a leadership role in the Catholic priesthood in the Americas. It was while preparing a sermon for Pentecost, in 1514, that the whole weight of the evil that was being perpetrated by the conquest and the resultant institution of slavery dawned in his consciousness. While preparing his sermon, *de Las Casas* found in the Bible, in the thirty-fourth chapter of Ecclesiastes, these stinging words:

230

> *The Most High is not pleased with the offerings of the*
> *wicked;*
> *neither is he pacified for sin by the multitude of*
> *sacrifices.*
> *The bread of the needy is their life;*
> *he that defraudeth him thereof is a man of blood.*
> *He that taketh away his neighbor's living slayeth him;*
> *and he that defraudeth the laborer of his hire is a*
> *shedder of blood.*

As *de Las Casas* read these words, a light from heaven seemed to shine on him and he realized that the system of slavery was wrong in principle. [51]

This man, the great apostle of the Indies, who lived to be ninety-two, was vigorous of temperament and intention. His

[51] Fisk, *The Discovery of America,* Houghton and Mifflin Co, Boston, 1892 p.450.

personality was irresistible, and he was very persuasive. For this reason he developed many enemies when he converted, became a priest and turned his back on the slave tradition. He became an important "lightening rod" of resistance in early attempts to reform the culture and style of Spanish conquest.[52]

De Las Casas was, on occasion, a personal councilor and chaplain to Commandant Hernan Cortez, the conqueror of the Aztec empire. An important reconnection is found between *de Las Casas* and Cortez in the reincarnation of Hernan Cortez as the president of the United States, Richard M. Nixon. (This is a separate study.) A close friend and personal spiritual councilor to the president, *Billy Graham* was often called to the White House to confer with, to counsel and to pray with Richard Nixon, who had been raised by a Quaker mother.

We find that this soul was also a reincarnation of *Bartholomew*, one of the twelve disciples of Jesus. This perhaps partially explains his profound religious charisma.

231

Bartholomew
Disciple of Jesus

Of the twelve disciples, *Bartholomew* was among the most quiet. His life was not given to any form of evangelism. He did not depart from his traditional Jewish cultural roots, al-

---

[52] The higher Self of Velasquez, who conquered Cuba in 1513, and whom de Las Casas opposed, is now reincarnated in Fidel Castro.

though he was "called." Nevertheless, his time would come in another life.

It was at the Pentecost celebration, after the crucifixion of Jesus, that a full realization of the meaning of salvation and resurrection entered the heart and mind of *Bartholomew*. At this Pentecost gathering of the faithful, he received the full empowerment of the Holy Spirit, as promised by Jesus. This spiritual event was an illumination according to the capacity of his soul.

Pentecost, as a call to righteousness, remained a symbolically important time in the life of *Bartoleme de Las Casas*. It was the time at which he received his first illumination. *Billy Graham's* lifelong evangelistic crusades, his call to spiritual reform, acceptance and salvation in Christ, originated from this first Pentecost. Its healing and transforming power is derived from the innermost heart of Pentecostal communion.

Master Zoroaster
Holy Mother Russia

This study, although it may be difficult for some, is intended to further explain the principle of spiritual progress among a karmically integrated people. It may seem incomplete, even vague, because higher reality is not a product of human history.

Once again, a spiritual master is one who has ascended in consciousness into the world of higher cause and is able to function consciously from this higher realm into all levels of evolving life, including that on earth. Once a soul has been made a pillar of the divine plan, why would he or she ever wish to leave? In fact, there is an inner core group of masters who attend to earth plane needs. Such masters, as part of their chosen dharma, continue to work with students on earth. When a master chooses to teach a particular people or follow a certain mission on earth, that collective or special purpose is greatly blessed.

In approximately 900 B.C., an arhat incarnated in Persia with the mission of bringing spiritual enlightenment and direction to the people of that time. He was called *Zoroaster.*[*]

233

Zoroaster
(c. 900 B.C.)

[*] Many historians place Zoroaster at 550 to 650 BC, the author believes the correct date to be three hundred years earlier.

Zoroaster received a noble education. However, after experiencing an inner awakening, he became troubled, saddened, even repelled by the spiritual corruption and ignorance of his time. This is often the experience of the great ones. He then retreated—some say into a cave—for many years, to gather higher spiritual vision and God-empowerment.

When *Zoroaster* returned to civilization, he came as an enlightened saint with great psychic powers. During those years of retreat, he had been the chosen disciple of an evolved angel. His teachings were primarily about angels and their relation to humanity and righteousness. He taught that the divine spirit was expressed in cosmic fire, manifested in the warmth of the sun. This fire had many levels of expression; it both purified the soul and destroyed the dross. Fire as a divine radiation became the symbol of purification rites for *Zoroasterians*. In all places of worship, a sacred flame was maintained to express the spirit of divine consciousness. Such fire symbols are still used as symbols of spiritual power in many Christian churches, as well as in most other churches in the form of candles; they are burned in memory of a loved one, or to light the way of a prayer.

234

On reentry into worldly life, *Zoroaster* went directly to the center of civil power on a mission to convert the king. The king was receptive, but the imperial priest and magicians resisted. *Zoroaster* was given an opportunity to meet these magicians before the king's assembly, in a great contest of spiritual powers. *Zoroaster's* ability to perform magic greatly exceeded that of the court magicians. As a result, the magicians were banished from court and *Zoroaster's* reformation was given full imperial authority.[53]

Zoroaster's life represents a true foundation in the spiritual history of the West. It is a great passion play in world collective memory, one that established many of the psychospiritual archetypes of early Judaism, Christianity and Islam. For example, the Bible story of Moses' meeting with the pharaoh's court magicians, and their defeat in a contest of magical powers, is an ar-

---

[53] Some of these same court magicians, those who resisted *Zoroaster's* reformation, later became perpetually trapped in an age-long (3,000 year) karmic cycle of resistance to any other opportunities for spiritual guidance from higher sources.

chetypal *Zoroastrian* story. The story of Moses was recorded around 690 B.C., by an inscribing process that was intended to create a Jewish version of the powerful magician Moses. Another example of this type of religious/literary license is found, as we have seen, in the Bible story of Daniel, which was written in approximately 170 B.C. Daniel's story is another psychospiritual rendition of the "holy prophet at court," unconsciously based on the original story of the great Persian religious reformer *Zoroaster*.

At the end of his life, *Zoroaster* ascended into the cosmic realms, taking his body with him, in front of witnesses. Although he was not yet a spiritual master, *Zoroaster* was empowered by the angel of the seventh ray. This empowerment permitted his publicly witnessed ascension. A similar example of empowerment is reflected in the Bible stories of the ascension of Elijah and Jesus, and later still in the story of Mohammed. It was even claimed that *Zoroaster* had a virgin mother.[54]

This soul is now one of the great spiritual masters of our planetary collective, on the seventh ray of expression. His abilities as a wielder of divine power are of the highest quality. In his last life on earth, in eighteenth century Europe, he achieved a union of material and spiritual influences that gave him physical immortality. The ability to ascend into higher dimensions, or to descend and manifest an earthly body at will, is a very rare expression of spiritual empowerment. Immortality of the lower human personality alone is impossible, as well as undesirable. However, after the ascension of mastery, the ability to create a physical body at will can serve a higher purpose. For example, it can be a practical demonstration to inspire students, or persons of influence such as the Persian king.

235

No spiritual master, however, would ever use such powers to achieve dominion over anyone. What is sometimes referred to as the "perfect law" of God embodies the principle of freedom in spiritual development. Any potent magician, (or politician or even salesman) who exercises psychic power over others—to dominate, confuse, extract profit or draw attention to himself in any

---

[54] A virgin mother is the *pure soul* in God. In ancient days it symbolized the belief that the soul of a great prophet was born of, and protected by, a guardian angel—an angel "Mother" from God.

way—is not led by the forces of light. The purpose of life on earth is spiritual evolution; this evolution is the Mother of all planetary life. Spiritual evolution can be helped along by those who would serve God, but they have no right to try to control the higher Selfhood, which is the legitimate domain of God.

In any study of early *Zoroastrianism*, it is important to note that, shortly after the life of this great teacher, the principles he expressed began to evolve into forms that he did not support.

Prince Rakoczi of Translyvania, Comte De St. Germain
(c. 1710 —unknown)

The former *Prince Rakoczi*, also called the *Comte De St. Germain*, or the *Master Rakoczi*, is the same soul who was *Zoroaster.* Some information about the life of this master can be found in old theosophical writings. In reviewing this material, it would be wise to be selective. Myth and misinformation surround the mysterious life and purpose of this great one. What is unspoken and unwritten is also important.

This spiritual master is now responsible for the future direction of the Russian collective. The karmic involvement of this great teacher with the inner history of the Russian collective will be more apparent from our next study, which reveals the progress of the peoples of the early Persian empire. When seen from the perspective of the Akashic Records, this connection reveals the perfection of the divine plan.

In the future, the Russian Orthodox Church will once again rise as a social institution of unprecedented political and economic influence under a renewed Christian impulse of benevolent spiritual inclusiveness. This inclusiveness will evolve from the highest level of spiritual comprehension and communion, which is quite above and beyond words. When all theosophistry, or intellectual theology, ends worship of God begins. The innate mysticism of the Russian people, guided by a spiritual master of the seventh ray, will eventually prevail in the great cause of spiritual reformation for Russia. Religious mysticism is Russia's gift. Prophetically speaking, this renewed religious union will help the Russian people achieve both spiritual and material empowerment. In time, a new form of money may evolve from the collective resources of the re-empowered Russian Orthodox Church.[55]

When worship of the divine spirit in Christic communion becomes the highest form of the collective expression, then the doctrines and dogmas of religion (or politics) will assume a secondary, non-exclusionary place in the Church. When words and ideas stop interfering with the light of God, and all hearts are invited to

---

[55] Yet another example of a social transformation impulse evolving from spiritual communion can be found in the social healing movement of Alcoholics Anonymous. (What does this have to do with *Zoroaster*? It is this: the primary impulse of original *Zoroastrianiam* was that of spiritual purification and sobriety; the original *Zoroastrians* were the prototype of the original Puritans.) It may seem trite, but the phenomenal present-day success of Alcoholics Anonymous in Russia, and its continuing spread in that needy society, represent a new ground of religious purification and reform for that people. We note the power of the socio-religious evangelism of Alcoholics Anonymous. This private and voluntary group work was first inspired as an answer to the prayers of two American alcoholics, a business man and a medical doctor, who helped each other to stay sober; the teachings of the resulting movement contain valid direction for achieving sobriety through spiritual renewal and purification. This same need is the spiritual testing ground for the general Russian public of today. Alcoholics Anonymous expresses the collective spirituality and the openness of a non-sectarian, non-fundamentalist, populous form of Christianity. It meets in private homes, or in Church buildings, or in public buildings, wherever an opportunity is made. Its form of help sometimes includes prayer and the laying on of hands (among the more religious groups). This religious type social work is an archetypal model that contains the "seed forms" of a religious purification movement necessary for a redefinition of the basic theology of the Russian Church.

unite in prayer and communal worship, a universal Christic Unity will be possible. This renewed spirit of inclusiveness will represent a willingness on the part of the Russian collective to embrace true social enlightenment. In time, the mystical prophecies about the future of Russia as holy Mother Russia—protector of the Christian faith—may come true.

238

Charlemagne
Archetype Prince of God's People

Tracking of a collective progression across time can be done by following the karmic course of powerful leadership. While tracking *Cyrus the Great*, the 550 B.C. Persian conqueror of Babylon, we find an example of a highly karmic soul, one who has become the bearer of an archetype. His karmic energy has become a soul magnet for collective spiritual progression.

Cyrus the Great
(c. 600 —529 B.C.)

The name *Cyrus* means "son" in a local dialect. Considered one of the great Persian conquerors of pre-Christian times, *Cyrus* was born as a noble in Persia, in northern Iran. He was trained as a military commander. Winning the enthusiastic support of his soldiers, he eventually planned and led a revolt against the domination of cruel territorial overlords. He went on to conquer all of the Persian and Mesopotamian lands, including most of present-day Turkey and some of lower Russia.

In council, after his conquests, *Cyrus* carefully considered the religious and cultural organization of his new empire. His choice was the continued rule of Zoroastrianism, in its pure Persian form. An intelligent administrator who listened to wisdom, *Cyrus* choose, for example, to be even-handed with the Jews when they petitioned the king to be allowed to retain their own religious faith, and with others who had supported him in his campaign against Babylon. His acknowledgment of each group, and of their rights, was recognized as good policy. Early Jews in Babylon, who were freed by *Cyrus* to practice their faith, called this Persian king a great messiah.

Cyrus was honored by his soldiers, even worshipped by some, as a sacred incarnation of the great sun god. Many of these soldiers were members of an early Mithric/Apollo sun-god warrior cult, a soldier society that performed Zoroastrian Mithric rites. These soldiers and most others at his court called *Cyrus* "Son-of-God," a title of reverence and respect.

As a matter of religious history, and for the purpose of this study, it is important to understand that all the books of the Old Testament (except the earliest version of the Torah, scribed around 650 B.C. in Jerusalem) were created in Babylon after 550 B.C., as religious plays or sermons. They were seen as contributions to a religious ferment that evolved in competition with Zoroastrian social reformation efforts. These Judeo-Babylonian writings included the Old Testament books of First and Second Samuel: the stories of King David and King Solomon.[56]

This soul has now become the carrier of one of the great archetypes of Western religious history that can be translated as "Prince of God's People" or, in biblical reference, as "King Saul of the Bible—Chosen Prince of the People." Through the continued calling forth of his person by his collective, and through his individual soul's response in future incarnations, he has become a representative karmic leader of an ongoing branch of the world collective.

As we shall see, in the five famous historical lives that this soul has lived, he has always returned to head—or, in the case of his last life, to teach—an empire or a people in the ongoing flow of biblical archetypal energy. His collective karma calls him to the front. His individual sense of duty empowers his expression, which includes an awareness of group welfare. A social leadership repetition is of-

---

[56] Samuel was the first historical religious play. It was a passion drama, written in the first person, called "I, Samuel" in its first presentation. This is important to know because the mythical personification of the Hebrew King Saul, portrayed in the Bible story of Samuel, had the *Persian King Cyrus* as a prototype.

ten born out of a strong karmic complex. This is the case with the former *Cyrus the Great*. Such a repetition expresses a leadership dharma that has been chosen on invisible spiritual levels to lead a massive wave of spiritual evolution. This is a good example of the karmic progression of a spirit-ordained, and spirit-maintained, soul group because it can be observed moving in and out of earth history, as an identifiable pattern of group reincarnation.

The soul of this "King of the North," as he is referred to in biblical myth, is not yet a spiritual initiate. As a soul, he is now becoming a well-established probationer on the path toward enlightenment. To understand the spiritual karma of this one, we can ask several intuitive questions: How is he guided? Who are his teachers? Which of the great ones support his progress and the progress of his collective? In what direction, and toward which ideals, will he lead his soul group? The great spiritual ideal that this soul must contend with is that of the anointed leadership of a "national kingdom under God." This old archetype represents a karmic question that lies at the root of the struggle of Christian monarchy: Was such a monarchy ever ordained by God?

In his next great public life, this soul reincarnated with many of his former followers in order to influence developing Christianity in a major way. He became *Constantine the Great*, the visionary Roman emperor who was the founder of the first Christian imperial state.

241

Constantine The Great
(c. 280—May 22, 337)

The life of *Constantine I* (*Constantine the Great*) is a pivotal study for the subsequent history of Christianity in the West and in the East. The son of a Roman Caesar, *Constantine* was drawn, over the course of civil wars and conquests, toward new forms of organized Christianity.

A full study of the ancient Zoroastrian roots of Mithraism is important to understand the fateful turn that Christianity took during this period. Older forms of Zoroastrianism had evolved into the rites of Mithraism. This type of worship of a solar deity had slowly merged with the Greco-Roman and Egyptian rites of Apollo. A creed developed from the new Mithric rites that supported a soldiers' cult: all for one, and one for all.

This archetype of fraternity has ancient roots in the collective unconscious. It is an archetype of spiritual family, of shared success and shared danger—including a sacred sacrifice—that must be allowed collective expression in a benevolent form because it represents a basic spiritual need. Earth is a planet of sacrifice. All forms, including the persona, are sacrificed to a higher purpose. This is the basic mystery of spiritual evolution. Certain aspects of early Christianity did, in fact, provide a benevolent interpretation of this truth. Original Christianity expressed the ideal of a brotherhood and sisterhood that unified its family members through such sacred symbols as the Eucharist, the sharing of bread and wine, and the sacrifice of Jesus as the Son of God.

242

With the emergence of the teachings of Jesus, certain members of the old Mithraic cult converted to a Christianized form of their old beliefs. The older form of the soldier cult of Mithra had a blood rite that involved the shedding of a sacred bull's blood. One of the Mithraic initiations was to be washed in the blood of the sacred bull as a symbol of the conquest of the material world.

Why is this important? Because, in the fourth century, many of the soldiers of this form of Christianity continued to believe that God can be represented in the earthly person of an emperor who is chosen of God. However, a Caesar, or earthly king, was not identified by Jesus as a potential leader for the coming kingdom of God on earth. According to Christ, only the power of God could be recognized and honored. This was the teaching of a pure theocracy, not involving the intercession of priests. However, in the mixed creed of Mithric Christianity, to fight as a soldier for a Caesar or an empire became a noble responsibility of the soldier-brotherhood in Christ (*miles Christi*). This Mithraism was the origin of the Christianized ideation that supported the soldier cults of the Christian medieval monarchies, such as the knights of the Crusades, and the knights of Malta. The archetypal story of a people choosing a king to rule them (e.g., King Saul of the *Book of Samuel*) is the repeated test in the rise of Christian monarchies during the Middle Ages, an anachronism in terms of the actual teachings of Jesus.

As we examine the Akashic Records with respect to the soldier societies and Christian warlords and monastic dynasties, we must regard these memories with passive indifference. We reach into the quiet place of release in our meditation. All public choices are karmic, but we need not share that karma by judging it. These types of choices, for battle or for capitulation, for war or for some alternative, are as old as humanity.

What is the Christ Light depiction of warfare? We recall a tale from one of the oldest religious books in recorded history, the Bhagavad-Gita. Krishna, another early Christ-personification archetype, says to his disciple Arjuna, who represents the archetype of the obedient warrior prince: "To live or to die in battle, to kill or to preserve the lives of others, is the domain of God. It is your responsibility to do your duty." All souls on the first ray of soul evolution view this as their primary spiritual responsibility.

243

We cannot attempt to give a shallow answer to the question of war or peace if we wish to retain any semblance of clarity of vision. Each soul will be tested with these types of choices. The choices of first-ray leadership at any given time in history are based on the needs of the many under a given set of circumstances. Which man can tell another what to do? We must simply observe these choices, pray for guidance and watch the karmic consequences over time. How much more can we do? Did Jesus tell the soldier not to soldier? No. He counseled him not to cheat and steal, nor to bare false witness. He told him that if he wished to live in eternal peace, to give up the world and worldliness, to surrender everything to divine guidance, and care for his neighbor. Perhaps that was saying that he should not soldier, but we cannot judge.

A sword, hilt up with the point down into the earth, was a symbol of the ancient Mithric rite in a military, pre-Christian form. This sword had an imperial crown on top and was similar to the symbol that *Constantine* is said to have seen in a dream. In this dream, supposedly before the battle that won him the empire, *Constantine* was told "by this sign you will conquer." A later depiction of *Constantine's* sign as a crowned cross was strikingly similar to the Mithric cross. With the help of this mythical-religious energy, and supported by loyal soldiers, both Christian and Mithric, Constantine established the first Christianized Roman administration in history. To this day, spiritually committed Christians argue the righteousness of this critical point in the path of the Church under Roman domination.

The time of *Constantine I* is the karmic root of both the Eastern and the Western Church of Christianity. Most of the psychic force of Roman Catholic mythology, and of all its Protestant breakaway sects, as well as Eastern Orthodoxy, began with, and proceeded forward from, the Christianized, imperialistic assumptions that came into power with *Constantine*. This became a great karmic burden—a nut, so to speak, that would take fifteen hundred years to crack. In any case, this strong soul was now in a karmic groove (a *samskara*) of great depth. The civil wars of the Roman Empire continued. Four hundred years later, this archetypal "Chosen Prince of God's People," again entered life to achieve great fame and influence. By accepting a life as *Charlemagne, King of the Franks,* this soul's karma as the "monarch anointed of God" (a title given to him by the people in several past lives) continued to grow.

244

When reviewing the life and times of *Charlemagne*, it is important to keep a detached perspective. In some ways, these events expressed progress for civilization, representing a salvation and protection from the piracy of warring states in Europe. In other ways, the land was invaded by a new wave of brutality. Brutality is as old as humankind. *Charlemagne,* son of a Frankish king, was born into a destiny with karmic roots as far back as the early Aryan invasions of the West, and even the pharaohs of Egypt.[57]

Charlemagne (Charles the Great)
(742—814)

Charlemagne was crowned the Holy Roman emperor on Christmas Day, in 800 A.D., by Pope Leo III. This fact, in itself, is of major importance on a karmic level. *Charlemagne*, as a secular Christian, was more interested in the Frankish conquest and settlement of the empire than in theology. He was brilliant but illiterate. Nevertheless, he developed an official position that supported literacy and intellectual development among his people. He sponsored education by founding a school to which he summoned scholars from around Europe. For example, the British scholar-monk Alcuin, whom *Charlemagne* appointed to head his school, was an arhat—a reincarnation of the former Gamaliel, grandson of Hillel, who was head of the Jerusalem Boys School during the life of Jesus, and who recognized Jesus, after the crucifixion, as the Messiah.

245

Charlemagne participated personally in the development of theological argument and ideation, as did *Constantine*, at the First Council of Nicaea. He impressed his ideals and beliefs on others,

---

[57] The degree of prejudice and mythology surrounding the life of *Charlemagne* is staggering. You are cautioned to see through the shallow surface of the historical reporting of that day, and to be aware of the histories written in centuries following. Men "appoint" heroes and surround them in mythology.

using the force of his person and stature. The *Carolingian* Renaissance was made possible, in great part, through his efforts and the efforts of the scholars and teachers he gathered to support his educational reforms. By attempting to build a better future for himself and his followers, *Charles* earned a better karma. In this sense, he was an important social reformer. The spiritual influence of Alcuin continued to work quietly on *Charlemagne*, revealing its effects on the king's character development two lifetimes later.

As a dictator of the civil order, *Charlemagne* developed a style of administration that allowed regional autonomy. Under his system of administration, Jews and others were relatively free to practice their beliefs, as long as all obeyed the few culturally standardizing laws.[58] From a military perspective, the style of *Charles'* conquest was merciless toward resisters. For example, after one battle, over seven hundred Saxons were executed. Decisions such as these, which may sound criminal, cannot be judged by today's standards. The Frankish style of warfare practiced by *Charlemagne* was neither better nor worse than every other former historical conquest—including the methods of Genghis Khan. The Mongol hordes were not more brutal than the Frankish hordes; charges of brutality often reflect the biases of a writer's perspective.

Most of human history can be interpreted in terms of guided or misguided leadership. What the world needs most is spiritually enlightened leadership. This is how basic human karma—personal, social or civil—continues to evolve. Unguided by enlightened vision, leadership is either good or evil, filled with high potential or disaster—all mixed in the same pot. For better or for worse, this is the "stew" of historical progress.

As a primary first-ray soul, *Charlemagne* took on a heavy karmic responsibility for the progress of the leadership impulse consigned to a mass of people. By continuing to choose the same leadership, this whole people choose to evolve to-

---

[58] This system of autonomous administration was very similar to how the conquest and administrative re-organization of the Persian empire was conducted by *Cyrus,* approximately 1,340 years earlier.

gether. We find him incarnating next in Russia as *Czar Peter the Great.*

His three preceding historical lives, as *Cyrus, Constantine,* and *Charlemagne,* clearly expressed the powerful, intermingled karmic complex at work in the life of the greatest reforming *Czar—Peter I of Russia.* Past events and former choices of this bearer of the archetype "Prince of the People" invisibly influenced events and circumstances in his life. Trapped in a public riot at age ten, the future Czar experienced the trauma of having a close advisor and protector killed while he clutched the boy's sleeve for protection. A weaker character might have been intimidated for life by such an experience. *Peter,* the "strong one," had the opposite reaction, perhaps equally unfortunately. A sense of merciless, preemptive action remained part of his psyche from that day on. Deeply scarred by that event, he moved toward greater violence. In time, *Peter* became a "soldier's commander," both loved and feared, but supported without question, by his troops.

247

Peter the Great of Russia   *Prince Peter Kropotkin*
(1672—1725)   *(1842—1921)*

In the course of his career, *Czar Peter* conquered new territory on the Baltic and on the Crimean coast for a new navy. He built the city of St. Petersburg, ostensibly named after Saint Peter, the "Rock" of Christianity, but also conveniently glorifying the Czar's name. These reforms were repetitious of events that manifested in the life of *Cyrus The Great of Persia,* as well as in the construction and renaming of the city of Constantinople, by

Constantine, which became the seat of government for the entire Roman Empire.

You could easily spend months reviewing these lives. The important thing is to invite into your study the higher perspective of spiritual intuition. You can meditate on the spiritual purpose of it all. What is the destiny of this soul? What will this people achieve in the world? What gifts may they be required to produce in support of the future of the human race? These questions can be answered, at least in part, with a review of Cza*r Peter's* next incarnation. He returned to the community of his chosen responsibility very shortly after his life as Czar, during a time of great intellectual and spiritual ferment. Bridging the nineteenth and twentieth centuries, he was born again as a Russian prince, and again inherited great wealth and power.

Perhaps due to better karma in this life, *Prince Peter Kropotkin* received a good education at a military academy—more education than he had received for many lifetimes—and later became an explorer and a world-renowned geologist. After traveling through Russia and Europe, he was recognized as a social philosopher and communitarian reformer. Loved and admired by many and hated by some, he once again emerged as a powerful leadership figure in Europe. He was a prince of his people, seeking "light" for their passage. The study of his life is like reading pure Russian romance.

248

As *Kropotkin*, this soul had a much happier childhood. However, as a prince of the old aristocracy, he was still born into a psychospiritual prison. At least, in this life, he no longer wished to be the prison's chief warden, or even a prison guard. The future welfare of the Russian people and the Russian monarchy, and the role of the Church in Russian society, were his life's work. All the personal challenges of this life were a direct result of his own past-life karmic making. He was forced to face, and correct, many of his former misguided actions.

At the end of the nineteenth century, intellectual and spiritual change was in the air worldwide. The psychospiritual atmosphere of the world was growing brighter; its radiance was beginning to shine everywhere. This was especially true in Czarist Russia, where light and dark forces stood out against a karmic background that was deeply entrenched in feudal domination and slavery. But social slavery cannot last forever. The morning of a new earth was dawning for mankind—or so said Swedenborg. In this new atmosphere, the higher spiritual capabilities of this strong soul began to awaken.

Prince Peter Kropotkin was both inspired and shamed by his new vision. He was influenced by such intellectuals as the French author Alexis de Tocqueville, who wrote *Democracy in America* (2 vols.; 1835, 1840). This shocking awakening inspired him to tend to Russia's cultural needs. He was drawn to champion a new political movement for Russia, one of social and economic freedom. A hundred years earlier, just such a movement had expressed itself fully in the minds of American intellectuals such as Jefferson, Franklin and Thomas Paine. These fathers of the American Revolution had helped the American Colonists throw off British feudal domination. It would not be so easy in Russia.

Prince Peter Kropotkin was also greatly influenced by Count Leo Tolstoy, one of the great initiates of the modern world. Regardless of how it may be interpreted on a personal level, Tolstoy's influence on *Kropotkin* was psychically potent. The relationship between these two continues to have a strong, although perhaps unconscious, collective influence on the future of Russia.

The nineteenth century was also the age of the New England transcendentalists, of Emerson, Alcott and Thoreau—some of whom had participated in the Carolingian Renaissance, or later European enlightenment.[59] This was a time of intellectual freedom and social experimentation (especially in America), including many attempts at communal living that were intended to lead to a higher order of society. *Kropotkin* attended the First Socialist International held in Paris. This gathering had its roots, metaphorically at least, in the First Council of Nicaea, and before that in Babylonian reform movements.

Thereafter, no matter what *Kropotkin* said, he was identified as a leader of early communism. His support for social freedom

---

[59] For example, the American social philosopher Bronson Alcott was a reincarnation of the teacher Alcuin.

led him to be associated in the public mind with the anarchist movement. In an attempt to discredit any political movement toward social freedom, the aristocracy and especially the organized Church, quickly identified anarchists as mad bombers and perpetrators of other destructive activities. After he became associated with both communists and anarchists, *Kropotkin* was excommunicated and even imprisoned for a time. He was forced to give up claim to his title and to his wealth and become a Russian expatriate. His continued activism after these early years is a fascinating study.

A socialist-anarchist cult grew up around *Kropotkin's* person. In France, he was lovingly called "Notre Pierre" (our Peter). Some of his writings include *Fields, Factories, and Workshops* (1899); *Mutual Aid* (1902); *The Great French Revolution* (1909) and *Ethics* (1924). He wrote about the state as the root of all evil, and argued that it must be eliminated. After the Bolshevik takeover, this father of the early Russian revolution was permitted to return to Moscow. He was allowed to roam freely and to speak his mind, although he remained outspokenly anti-Bolshevik for the rest of his life. It is likely that the Bolsheviks feared him.

Kropotkin's inner transformational process can be interpreted as a healthy response to the death of "Saul," and as a necessary New Age dissolution of the ancient archetype of the "King of God's People." "The prince of this world shall not enter the kingdom of God": in the light of this saying, is it not time to retire the archetype of "prince"? Indeed, it was time for this soul to be freed—if he could accomplish it—to take his place as a participant within the communion of humanity, as a brother, student, teacher or friend.

Catherine the Great
Stewardship of Bondage

Peter the Great resolved that each Czar would appoint his successor. Thus, the leadership of Russia would not be left to the whims of family inheritance. This system had been used by Roman Caesars many centuries earlier. However, Peter failed to follow his own plan; he died unexpectedly, probably of pneumonia, without appointing his successor. Instead, karma and divine destiny took a hand.

Frustrated after several years of aristocratic mismanagement, the remnants of Peter's imperial guard helped Elizabeth, Peter's daughter, become empress of Russia. Elizabeth's nephew Peter, who became Peter III on his aunt's death, was married to *Catherine*, daughter of the German prince of Anhalt-Zerbst, from Poland. Again with the help of the imperial guard, *Catherine* deposed her husband (although it is likely that she did not participate consciously in the murder of her husband). Upon Czar Peter III's death, *Catherine* became the sole ruler, *Empress Catherine II, Czarina*.

251

Hatshepsut
(reigned c.1472—1458 B.C.)

Catherine the Great
(May 2, 1729—Dec. 25, 1761)

We find an interesting past-life connection with ancient Egypt. *Catherine the Great of Russia* was an incarnation of *Egyptian Queen Hatshepsut*, who battled her step-son, Thutmose III, for control of the Egyptian throne. That life makes an interesting study. Czar Peter III of Russia was not the same soul as Thutmose III, yet the karmic complex that came home to roost for this queen of Russia, and for the Russian people, had deep karmic roots in the eighteenth dynasty of ancient Egypt.

In another life in the fourth century B.C., the soul of *Catherine* was the wife of a Persian prince. Thus, as a karmic noble woman, she was following her destiny as a natural leader of a collective that progressed out of ancient Egypt, through Persia and eventually into eighteenth century Russia. This study reveals a karmic "bitter root" beneath modern-day Russian social dilemmas. This "bitter root" leads back to the biblical times of imperial Egypt, and the archetypal prayer associated with it is: "Let My People Go."

A review of the life and times of *Catherine the Great* helps us better understand present-day Russia. The vision, direction and will of the leadership of eighteenth century Russia were controlled by the karmic perspectives of feudal domination and serfdom. *Catherine* was a talented, reform-minded queen and her reign strengthened Russia as an imperial state. She was a strong woman, who continued the slow reformation begun by her grand uncle-in-law, *Peter the Great*, that was to bring Russia into the modern world, while retaining control over most of the wealth of the vast Russian empire, and all its power. Her intentions, within the framework of her understanding, were benevolent; she was as much a victim of her karmic condition as were the people under her feudal power.

The life of a soul such as hers can only be judged by its own merits—not by the failures or tragedies of the entire collective into which *Princess Catherine* was thrown at the age of fifteen. From a positive perspective, *Catherine the Great* was a patron of the arts as well as a sponsor of educational reform. Under her patronage, for example, the University of Moscow and the Russian Academy of Science grew to become internationally respected centers of learning. *Catherine* was also a prolific writer who permitted, for the first time in Russian history, private printing presses and relaxed censorship laws. She was a liberal in some ways and a conservative in other ways.

Most of *Catherine's* constructive contributions can be interpreted in terms of idealistic self-interest. Although intending social progress, she wished to retain control over her reforms and over the power of her office. In this, she demonstrated little understanding about universal freedom. Pugachev's revolt caused *Catherine* to expand some reforms for the serfs. However, the old Russian aristocracy's backlash toward that reform led her to reverse her position and consent to greater aristocratic control over the serf population. Whether *Catherine* could have prevented these renewed social repressions is hard to say.

We have a follow-up study on *Catherine*. This soul is now living in twentieth century North America. She was born in Canada in the late 1950s. Following her natural talent, she earned a doctorate in the field of education, and became a respected educator. This present incarnation represents an anonymous life of karmic rest. The fact that she has reincarnated into a pleasant life indicates an element of goodness and grace protecting her individual soul's progression.

Gorbachev and Kissinger
The Theme of Leadership

To help us further understand the complexity of the karmic dilemma of eighteenth century Russian leadership, we will add two
other past-life traces to this study. Both of these souls were influential intellectuals; both were still cloaked in psychic resistance
and separation from the light of God. Both are well-known in our
time and are still active on the world stage. One of these was
involved in the leadership of an early Russian peasant revolt; the
other was a powerful personal advisor to Empress Catherine. Both,
for a time, wielded sufficient power to affect the social climate of
eighteenth century Russia. Today they are two different, yet similar, men of personal influence and power: *Mikhail Gorbachev*
and *Henry Kissinger.*

Mikhail Gorbachev
(Mar. 2, 1931—)

Yemelian Pugachev
(c.1742—Jan. 22, 1775)

The soul of *Mikhail Gorbachev* was the former *Yemelian
Pugachev*, who in 1773 led a peasant revolt in Russia. A Don
Cossack, *Pugachev* declared himself to be Czar Peter III. Claim-
ing that he had lived through a botched murder attempt on his
life, this clever revolutionist declared an end to serfdom and a
revolt against Moscow. *Pugachev's* rebellion succeeded for a while
in Eastern Russia. He eventually descended on Moscow with an
army of 30,000. Catherine's forces defeated the peasant rebel-

lion and *Pugachev*, who was carried to Moscow in a cage, was beheaded.

A history of *Mikhail Gorbachev* needs no introduction. This former KGB officer was made head of the Communist Party in 1985. As president of the Soviet Union, frustrated by the status quo, he declared a new policy of *Glasnost* and *Perestroika*. *Gorbachev* was the last president of the old USSR. His present-day activities are mostly international. Often staying in New York City and San Francisco, he continues to travel around the world as a well-paid lecturer and representative of what some call the "new world order."

Grigory Potemkin
(Sept. 24, 1739—Oct. 16, 1791)

Henry A. Kissinger
(May 27, 1923—)

255

Another former star of eighteenth century Russian society, *Grigory Potemkin*, a personal advisor to Catherine the Great, reincarnated as *Henry A. Kissinger*. *Grigory Potemkin*, as a young officer of the imperial guard, helped Catherine II seize power. As an independent, preemptive decision by some of the officers of the imperial guard who were dissatisfied with weak rule, he may have helped arrange the demise of Catherine's husband, Czar Peter. Witty and intelligent, he had a strangely charismatic effect on Empress Catherine, *Potemkin* became one of her favorites, and remained her most trusted and, thus, most powerful advisor until the late 1780s, *Potemkin* used his position to advantage. He became one of the richest men in Russia.

The soul of *Grigory Potemkin* reincarnated in the twentieth century as *Henry A. Kissinger*. Born in Furth, Germany,

Kissinger's family migrated to the United States in 1938. In 1943, he became a U.S. citizen. Joining the American army, he served as an intelligence officer in the postwar U.S. military government of Germany. After the war, he studied at Harvard and earned a Ph.D. in political science. Serving as an advisor to the leadership of the new corporate world order, Kissinger was eventually assigned by the Rockefeller/Internationalist brain trust to become President Richard Nixon's chief foreign policy advisor. Establishing intellectual dominance over Richard Nixon, *Kissinger* was made U.S. Secretary of State. He served in this position under both Presidents Nixon and Ford. We note that President Ford's appointed vice president (after the resignation of Nixon) was a Rockefeller insider and family member, Nelson A. Rockefeller—formerly Pope Leo X.

Kissinger attained enormous political and economic power and prestige. Among *Kissinger's* achievements was the restoration of U.S. relations with the People's Republic of China. In the current phase of his career, he has negotiated himself into a position as the head of an extremely influential corporate consulting firm that does business in China. It is said that corporate insiders from the United States who wish to do business with China, do it through *Henry Kissinger and Associates*. With this latest development as a corporate power broker, *Kissinger* may be on his way to becoming, again, one of the wealthiest men in the world.

Why is any of this detail important? Well, the fact is, it really is not all that important. What is important for a serious student of Akashic history to learn is the fundamental premise of karmic repetition. The karmic wheel of repetition includes individuals and groups on every level of practical life. With this perspective, we see that the lives and choices of these highly karmic incarnations are set in a repetitive groove. It is the natural karma of former wielders of political power to continue to repeat their willful grasp for authority and riches until some higher force enlightens them.

Senmut, Hatshepsut's steward
(c.1450—c.1485 B.C.)

We can gain insight into the charismatic influence of *Potemkin* on Catherine by examining the connection between these two in ancient Egypt. Pharaoh Hatshepsut had an advisor named *Senmut*, whose name is inscribed in her royal tomb. Egyptologists assure us that *Senmut* most likely broke the law by surreptitiously placing his own name in a royal tomb. By scribing his name and indicating that he was *Hatshepsut's* favorite scribe and steward, it is likely that he believed he could preserve his *ka*, his soul, for all eternity. *Senmut* believed he would be allowed to live forever as the favored advisor to this royal court. The magic that Egyptians used was not without power; something seems to have worked as *Senmut* hoped. What is the old saying? "Be careful what you ask for; you might get it."

The same soul who became *Senmut* became *Potemkin*, who became *Kissinger*. In-between, there were a few other lives of little historical significance. The important pattern demonstrated in this progression is that power is a strong karmic repetition compulsion.

Aleksandr Solzhenitsyn
A Spiritual Mission to Russia

Due to the nature of this study, which involves current events of great importance, it is one of the more difficult cases to present with its full content and meaning. Our subject is the Russian author, political activist and recipient of the Nobel Peace Prize, *Aleksandr Solzhenitsyn*. He has attracted great controversy worldwide. Many people love him and many hate him. Of those who fear *Solzhenitsyn's* potential influence with the Russian people, most try to ignore him, or to pretend that his writing is not important for evolving Russian society. The purpose of this study is to present some insight into this arhat's mission to Russia.

Aleksandr Solzhenitsyn is one of the great arhats of planet Earth. In several former, historically famous, lives of tremendous social influence, he established a deep resonance in the psyche of the world collective. By doing research on these lives, you can see the connective karmic threads. It is important to remember that an arhat is a condition of the soul that is not always evident in the details of a particular incarnation. The real power of an arhat is his psychospiritual, and often unconscious, impact on the greater social collective.

258

The higher mental and spiritual power of a great soul is such that his social successes or failures imprint the very fabric of collective karma. An arhat must choose his way—sometimes blindly—depending on the karmic depth of the problem at hand. An arhat is inevitably a leader who shows the right direction to a people. He is the most important "seed" person in the forward movement of cultural transformation. He is not always exactly right but, karmically speaking, an arhat is never wrong. To resist the general spirit of an arhat's efforts is to choose a retrograde energy.

All souls who serve God, especially initiates, must seek to identify a great soul and to lend support to his proposed goals—or at least not to resist his vision. A search of Akashic history demonstrates, time and time again, that anyone who resists the transformation energy of an arhat invites a karmic disaster that will affect them for many future lifetimes. Those who follow the lead of an arhat, and choose to serve his cause, are safely held in the fold of spiritual protection. Words can not fully express the importance of this principle.

Aleksandr Solzhenitsyn
(Dec. 11, 1918—)

Solon, Greek legislator
(c. 639—c. 559 BC)

The progression of five famous lives led by the soul of *Solzhenitsyn* tell the story. This is another carrier of an archetype—a first-ray soul who carries the metaphoric designation of the "Legislator." A cultural subarchetype for him is "Aaron, Brother of Moses." In a past life as the Greek poet and philosopher *Solon*, he also earned the title of the "Liberator."

259

We know of *Solon* from his poetry. In approximately 600 B.C., ancient Athens was in political crisis. *Solon* was elected and given absolute power to legislate a solution. He canceled all debts and forbade debt-slavery. Political re-enfranchisement was made a function of talent, prosperity and wealth, rather than mere birth. By this action, *Solon* earned many enemies among the former slave owners and hereditary aristocracy.

Solon's solutions are not necessarily applicable to modern times, but the karmic remnant of his leadership from that life can be identified in his next incarnations.

As *Meng-tse*, the famous Confucian scholar of 300 B.C., this soul's entire life was spent studying and teaching the way of sociopolitical righteousness. *Meng-tse* is still lovingly referred to as "Great Legislator" by some present-day Confucians. As a follower of Confucius, *Meng-tse* aligned himself with the work of one of the world's greatest souls, the former Confucius, Kung Fu Tse.[60]

Meng-tse, whose moral strength could "bridge heaven and earth," focused on right action in the social realm. His philosophical focus was both highly spiritual and also practical and political. He refused to drift too far into mysticism, which could leave the people without right guidance from enlightened souls if they retreated from social activism.

The soul of *Meng-tse*, or *Mencius* as he was known in Latin, reincarnated in Rome as the *Emperor Marcus Aurelius*. These lives, when seen together, contribute to the observation that this soul may be one of the greatest social/philosopher leaders of all humanity, in terms of his accumulative historical contribution and cultural influence.

260

Meng-tse—Mencius
(c. 372—c. 289 BC)

In that next life, which carried him to the height of Roman society, this great soul was ushered in by the force of karmic magnetism to fulfill a role as a philosopher king of Rome. This

---

[60] Confucius, after a last life in Greece, c. 300 B.C., as a founder of Stoicism, has now become a first ray spiritual master. He is also another archetypal "Moses" figure.

was a Platonic concept that was embraced by many Roman idealists of that time.

The life of Roman *Emperor Marcus Aurelius*—while perhaps a success in terms of world literature (he is best known for his classic *Meditations* on Stoic philosophy)—was actually a life of great tragedy, of personal burden and pain. *Marcus Aurelius'* focus on the righteous administration of the Roman Empire was a direct karmic extension of this soul's past-life work as *Meng-tse*, of China.

Although the practical life of *Aurelius* was consumed by the tragedies of war, he persevered in holding to the highest ideals. The Christians against whom he spoke out, and later fought against, did not belong to the original communion from the stream of spirit idealized by Jesus. To say that *Aurelius* moved against Christians is not to conclude that he moved against Christ. This is a part of his life that must be carefully considered. To *Aurelius,* these early Christians were evading social responsibility. He wrote to correct them, much as *Meng-tse* condemned the social-separatist sects of his day.

Still working with older karmic streams and the retrograde difficulty that was Rome, *Aurelius* attempted to serve what he conceived of as his duty—to serve the best direction for Roman social stability. He was overwhelmed with the magnitude of that chore. In fact, this life as *Marcus Aurelieus* could be considered a karmic "overload." This great soul could not prevail within these difficult conditions and he retreated into his meditations. The ideal of imperial Rome, with its principles of territorial dominance and legalized slavery, was—even at its height—a failure.

But what of the karmic course of *Marcus Aurelius*? What became of him? This "seed man," the great idealist of righteousness, was given a second chance to bring right leadership and moral rule to the people. This arhat appeared again on the stage of world events as the American Civil War president *Abraham Lincoln.*

Marcus Aurelius
(Apr. 26, 121—March 17, 180)

Abraham Lincoln
(Feb. 12, 1809—Apr. 15, 1865)

The life of *Abraham Lincoln* cannot be fully understood without seeing it in the context of a major world event. Some historians believe that *Lincoln* was the greatest American president. The reality may be somewhat different, because he chose a path of war. But this is not easily analyzed. Perhaps *Lincoln's* greatest importance was as a leader who worked outside the law of the land. His was a brave and dangerous choice of action in terms of personal karmic consequence. The collapse of the union of the United States gave *Lincoln* a window of opportunity to enact some needed legislative changes for that union. His presidency during the Civil War, and his leadership during the threat of war, became a group initiatory experience for the people of both the Northern and Southern states. It was a course with desperate consequences.

The American Constitution was finalized against the objections of both Franklin and Paine—both great souls and guardians of the American independence movement. Despite their protest, legalized slavery was included as a protected condition of the Constitution. Slavery was the poisonous seed that had been encased in American Constitutional law, and that had to be removed. With the ratification of the Constitution in 1786, radical changes in that union became inevitable.

Thus, in the course of time—sixty years later—another arhat, the *"Legislator,"* was sent into incarnation, to face the test of civil collapse and help shepherd the American people through the dark times at hand. Indeed, the events of the American Civil War brought the American experiment to a time of choice—to a major spiritual crossroads—and almost to an end.

At this moment in history, our arhat appeared in the spiritually most unlikely place—as president of the United States. Think about this: if this soul had not been a former emperor of Rome, his election to the presidency of the United States would have been karmically unlikely, even impossible. Why? Because the karma of kings attracts and expresses political charisma. Little else can lead to political success. Thus, we see that even past personal disasters, such as an imperial Roman emperorship, can have constructive future karmic usefulness. This is an example of how spiritual dharma evolves over time.

Events between the American states began to heat up. With the Civil War already in full swing, *Lincoln* reluctantly wrote and signed the Emancipation Proclamation. Using the prestige of his presidential position against all the rules of the old legislative order, he emancipated those slaves currently in states in rebellion. Eventually this led to ex-slaves being admitted into paid service with the Union army.

Lincoln made a series of profound moral choices of great collective consequence. In order to gain a deeper understanding of the issues involved, and of the role of *Lincoln* in the American Civil War, additional study is recommended. With hindsight, it may be easy to conclude that war is not a good way to solve anything because there is always a terrible spiritual price to pay. But here is the problem: it is difficult to tell if *Lincoln* felt that he had a choice in the matter. The complexity of the problem was increased by the willingness of some foreign powers to side with the South to protect their financial interests in loans to the Southern cotton industry. Some European colonial powers were even tempted by a vision of the re-conquest of Western lands. It is said that Russia's Czar, Alexander II, who ceded Alaska to the United States in 1867, supported *Lincoln* in his efforts. The Czar issued a diplomatic communiqué to several European nations stating that military intervention in the American Civil War would be considered an act of war against Russia. That is a part of history that remains unacknowledged to this day. The possible threat from England, Spain or even France led *Lincoln* to believe he had to make a choice between possible evils. It was a no-win dilemma that was fully karmic, no matter what was chosen.

Five days after the surrender of the Southern General Robert E. Lee, *Abraham Lincoln* was shot and killed while attending a play on the evening of Good Friday, two days before Easter. This was a highly symbolic time. We recall that the assassin was John Wilkes Booth, who soon reincarnated in Russia as the brother of a young revolutionary who was hanged after being caught in an assassination plot against the Czar. Vladimir Lenin, the former John Wilkes Booth, went on to become the brilliant but controversial leader of the future Soviet Union.

Abraham Lincoln intuited the inevitability of his possible death by assassination. It had been revealed to him in dreams. He accepted his death long before it happened. Perhaps a death wish had entered him unconsciously. He was greatly burdened by the tragedy of the war. Two years earlier, 50,000 soldiers from both the North and South had died in a single battle at Gettysburg. While riding his horse across the field where this great battle had been fought, *Lincoln's* personal ego-reserve shattered, leaving a painful, unhealed wound in his psyche.

His realization of the scope of the disaster of that war precipitated a profound moodiness in the emotions of the president. After that day, *Lincoln* no longer lived as a proud man. The weight of his role in the war began to press on him. His Gettysburg Address, displayed at the Lincoln Memorial in Washington D.C., is one of the most beautiful pieces of inspirational prose ever written. That short speech, delivered at Gettysburg to memorialize the battle, was a universal prayer for a nation, a prayer for humanity and a prayer for himself—as well as a prayer for all the soldiers who died in the conflict. *Lincoln's* assassination on Good Friday can be interpreted as a symbolic metaphor of submission to God, and an identification with the archetypal crucifixion of Christ. Perhaps the timing of his death even acknowledged a communion with the spirit of the martyrs of early Rome.

Post-Civil War history would have been different if *Lincoln* had lived to be elected for another term of four years. This would have enabled him to follow through with the economic, democratic reconstruction reforms he had in mind. Instead, after *Lincoln's* death, with political power brokers manipulating the congressional caucus and the electoral college, a series of weak presidents was selected. The worst of these was General Ulysses S. Grant, the former Civil War hero who had defeated General Lee.[61]

A drunken president such as Grant could be easily molded and used by sophisticated power brokers. This made it possible for greedy economic interests to continue to suppress the Southern states long after the war. They bought up cheapened land and created new forms of aggressive, military-backed, elitist economic monopolies—such as unrestrained private railroad monopolies. The result was the slaughter of millions of buffalo, the suppression of the North American natives and the inequitable division of conquered lands. This style of economic conquest was followed by the so-called robber barons, who used the government and military to further their own unethical economic schemes. Such unprincipled men had no trouble taking advantage of a war-weakened country, without regard for the public good.

The potential for this type of sociopolitical problem, interestingly, is emerging, in many ways, in Russia. Russia is now at an important turning point in social and political history. Will the Russian people be able to respond to the call for renewed collective responsibility? Will they be able to pull together with a constructive national patriotism for responsible social and economic reform? Or will they again be torn apart by overwhelming forces

[61] In a previous life, Grant had been a seventeenth century Ukrainian war leader who had, along with his army, pledged loyalty to the Russian Czar. As a *curio*, this same soul is now in incarnation, again in the U.S. He served in the 1970s as a captain in the U.S. army in the Vietnam conflict. This former president of the U. S. has, in this life, since Vietnam, made a simple life as a carpenter; his biggest battle now is with a whiskey bottle.

of greed, elitist power brokerage and by the inevitable political corruption that accompanies such power?

The great soul who was *Abraham Lincoln* has gone to Russia to try, again, to address this problem. After his difficult life as *Lincoln,* this soul could have returned forever to the embrace of the higher worlds to achieve spiritual mastery. But it appears that he chose instead to participate again in the cause of human civilization. This he is now attempting to do as the Russian writer, political-philosopher, social activist and leader *Aleksandr Isayevich Solzhenitsyn.*

In this present life as *Solzhenitsyn,* armed with *Lincoln's* unfinished ideals, this soul continues to do battle with forces of darkness and ignorance by spiritual-intellectual means. The battlefield for Russia's future is of the heart and the mind. Ideas, after all, have great power; by their right use, life can be won and a good future chosen. Furthermore, the relationship between Russia and the United States is spiritually intertwined. What affects one, tends to also affect the other.

Ralph Waldo Emerson
Christian Enlightenment

In this study, we trace the progress of one who, in many ways, can be considered a representative of the best intentions of early Christian enlightenment. We begin with the life of *Jerome*. He had two important, but anonymous, former incarnations of influential scholarly leadership, one as a chief librarian in Alexandria, Egypt, around 260 B.C., and another as a direct disciple of Confucius in China around 400 B.C.

St. Jerome
(340—420)

As an ascetic, intellectual youth, born to a wealthy Christian family, *Eusebius Hieronymus* studied the Roman classics. While still very young, he experience a "call" to the faith. By the age of nineteen, he had traveled to several Christian monastic centers of learning, meeting others of the new enlightenment. Later in life, after taking the name *Jerome,* he became a leader and scholar in the early Christian community, even serving for a while as secretary to the Bishop of Rome, Pope Damasus I.

Jerome's greatest work was the translation of the Bible into Latin, a text known as the *Vulgate*. A Father of Christianity and an official doctor of the Church, *Jerome* set a high moral and ethical standard for early Christian theology. The life of this gentle scholar continued to influence the course of developing Christendom for many centuries, in both the East and West. An advocate of moderate humanism, *Jerome* was an important cultural bridgeworker.

This soul reincarnated as the controversial Dutch educator, theologian and Aristotelian classicist, *Desiderius Erasmus of Rotterdam*—one of the greatest literary figures of the sixteenth century northern European Renaissance. A skilled social critic, *Erasmus* was both a theologian and a social philosopher. He became famous as the author of *In Praise of Folly*, a commentary on the foolishness of human pretension.

During the course of his life, *Erasmus* traveled to many centers of learning, as did *Jerome*. He was a friend and councilor to scholars and kings. He lived during the early Protestant Reformation, a time of the breakdown and recreation of European cultural values. Although he was an outspoken evangelist for social and religious reformation, this true initiate advocated a conservative approach—on the side of Christian moderation and restraint.

An outspoken critic of Church abuses, *Erasmus* also spoke in favor of cultural and theological unity. He supported the continued use of Latin as a unifying force in the Church, and in European culture. One of the great linguists and classicists of his age, he also produced a new translation of the *New Testament* from original Greek sources, thus returning to an impulse from his life as *Jerome*.

268

Desiderius Erasmus of Rotterdam　　*Ralph Waldo Emerson*
(c. 1466—July 12, 1536)　　*(May 25, 1803—Apr. 27, 1882)*

In his next life, the former *Jerome/Erasmus* reincarnated in the United States as *Ralph Waldo Emerson*, the son of a Christian

Unitarian minister, in Boston, Massachusetts. He re-entered the stream of public life in the nineteenth century, once again becoming a spiritual reformation influence for his generation. *Ralph Waldo Emerson* was a renowned American transcendentalist, essayist, lecturer, poet and philosopher. His influence was that of a pivotal mediator and spiritual father in the emerging nineteenth century American spiritual-intellectual renaissance.

A careful study of *Emerson's* life offers a healing experience for both the mind and emotions. An example of a third-ray initiate (the ray of philosophy and synthesis of thought), this humanitarian genius, social bridgeworker and advocate of social enlightenment, left an indelible imprint—as he had in several previous lives—on the psyche of his time.

The basic teaching of transcendentalism does not conflict with the true spirit and meaning of the teachings of the Christic illumination, as revealed in the life of Jesus. Much of *Emerson's* influence was to correct Christian misconceptions and superstitions. His life and work was clearly an extension of spiritual endeavors from the life of *Erasmus*.

A man ahead of his times in many ways, *Emerson* maintained a lifelong, healthy attitude of reciprocal helpfulness and social support toward all persons. This was especially true toward the cause of women's education. An advocate of interdependent world peace, based on personal freedom and empowerment, as well as individual and collective self-reliance, *Emerson* made himself a student of world politics, world literature and world religion. This intellectual outreach demonstrated his soul's sensitivity to higher guidance and direction.

In 1836, *Emerson* helped found the New England Transcendental Club. With this group effort, he also helped develop a public lecture guild that supported a philosophical platform called the Lyceum. The Lyceum was designed in the ancient Greek tradition as a public forum for academic free speech, education and public debate.

Also in 1836, *Emerson* published *Nature*, a book that expanded on the universalist transcendentalist theme that the organic basis of life, the function of all of nature itself, is a visible expression of higher spiritual truths.[62] In 1840, *Emerson* co-founded a transcendentalist magazine, *The Dial*, with his friend Margaret Fuller.[63] From that time, his fame as an author and lecturer grew worldwide. By 1850, he was often and lovingly referred to as the "Sage of Concord." *Emerson's* was a life dedicated to public goodness.

So how do we recognize initiates when they work within society? The answer is still the same: "By their fruits you shall know them." Everyone who enters an earth life is responsible for recognizing the truth and choosing to aid the highest leadership he can identify. Sometimes this is difficult since the higher voice has been outshouted by the lower voice. Thus, discrimination is important. Our spiritual leaders, the true initiates, the true elder brothers and sisters, are often not those given credit by the general public.

Personal talent is not synonymous with spiritual awakening. *Emerson* had many lives of intellectual-spiritual development, but that background does not define his spiritual status as an initiate. His character was gentle, but that still does not define the higher alignment of his soul. The attainment of initiation, the anointing in God, is a fact of soul—above and beyond all skills of the personality.

It is unlikely that this soul will incarnate on earth again within the next two centuries. If we were to speculate on the prophetic flow of the emergence of the consciousness of a New Age and a new people in South America, beginning in a couple hundred years, in a five-hundred mile radius around Lake Titicaca, we could look for his return in that direction.

But that is another story.

For now, it is enough.

---

[62] *Emerson's* intellectual premise in *Nature* may be a good example of the karmic correction of a past-life oversight.

[63] She was the great aunt of Buckminster Fuller, the famous American social visionary, structural engineer and inventor of geodesic domes, among other things.

Postscript

I would like to develop a collection of general questions on the subject of the Akashic Records, and on the nature of the inner spiritual life. Thus, I would very much like to hear from you, and to receive your gift of a good question, so that I can weave them into future presentations.

If you have any questions or comments concerning *Past Lives of Famous People,* that could be of interest to you or to others, please write directly to:

David Bengtson, 306-N W. El Norte Pkwy, Suite #1, Escondido, Calif., 92026

For my current e-mail address, please check in author's information on my publisher's web site: http://www.bluestar.com.

Please understand that I do not do personal readings, nor do I gather specific information on request from the Akashic Records. Therefore, keep your questions as general as possible, and keep them spiritual or historical in nature. Any subject of general interest would be appreciated. For example: what can we discuss about the nature of the Akashic Records, or the higher planes, or dimensions of consciousness, or the initiations, or about the general movement of social evolution on the worldly plane of history? On which subjects would you like more commentary? Please let me know.

A-Z Lives